WOMAN IN THE
NINETEENTH CENTURY

L.

Alphra Behn   *Oroonoko: or, The Royal Slave* (a novel)   N702

Margaret Fuller   *Woman in the Nineteenth Century*   N615

George Gissing   *The Odd Women* (a novel)   N610

Karen Horney   *Feminine Psychology*   N686

Raden Adjeng Kartini   *Letters of a Javanese Princess*   N207

Ruth Landes   *The Ojibwa Woman*   N574

George Meredith   *Diana of the Crossways* (a novel)   N700

May Sarton   *Mrs. Stevens Hears the Mermaids Singing* (a novel) N762

George Bernard Shaw   *An Unsocial Socialist* (a novel)   N660

Julia Cherry Spruill   *Women's Life and Work in the Southern Colonies*   N662

Barbara Bellow Watson   *A Shavian Guide to the Intelligent Woman*   N640

Mary Wollstonecraft   *Maria, or The Wrongs of Woman*   N761

Mary Wollstonecraft   *A Vindication of the Rights of Woman*   N373

WOMAN

in the

Nineteenth Century

Margaret Fuller

WITH AN INTRODUCTION
By Bernard Rosenthal

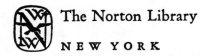 The Norton Library

NEW YORK

W · W · NORTON & COMPANY · INC ·

PRINTED IN THE UNITED STATES OF AMERICA

3 4 5 6 7 8 9 0

CONTENTS.

INTRODUCTION.

In its outlines, the life of Margaret Fuller (1810–1850) reads like an invented romance. Raised in a New England culture that assumed the intellectual inferiority of women, Margaret Fuller was rigorously educated by a stern though loving father who put into her head the heretical notion that girls were the intellectual equals of boys. Margaret Fuller acted upon this assumption throughout her life, sometimes with a sense of intellectual confidence that bordered on arrogance, as exemplified by her assertion while dining with Ralph Waldo Emerson, once her idol, that "I now know all the people worth knowing in America, and I find no intellect comparable to my own." Immodest though the statement may have been, it was made by a woman who had indeed conversed on at least equal terms with the intellectual élite of New England.

Among those whom she knew were such noted "transcendentalists" as Henry David Thoreau, Frederick Hedge, Theodore Parker, Bronson Alcott, and Orestes Brownson, to name a few. When it came time to find an individual who would edit *The Dial*, which lasted from 1840 to 1844, Margaret Fuller was the only one ready for the task. To be sure, some of her associates assumed that she would faithfully shape a journal that accorded with their own sense of "transcendentalism," but in this they would be disappointed. In spite of enormous pressures, she maintained full editorial control over the contents of the journal during the two years of her editorship. Brushing aside most attempts to influence her direction of the journal, she emphasized art over philosophy, the reverse of what Emerson did when he became editor after Margaret Fuller decided to resign. Before that time, however, she had used *The Dial* to promote German Romanticism, particularly the writings of Goethe; to express her literary and social theories; and to experiment with her own literary forms. Indeed, the actual volume of her contributions sometimes included more than half the contents of the journal. This emphasis on her own writings was not due to a lack of material, since she rejected numerous submissions urged upon her by Emerson and others. *The Dial*, so often thought of as the journal of American "transcendentalism," was, during her editorship, the journal of Margaret Fuller. This assertiveness had been typical of her from the time in 1836, when as an obscure young woman she had managed an invitation to visit the famous Emerson, until 1843 when she left *The Dial* and New England culture forever. It would continue throughout her life.

In 1844, having attracted the attention of Horace Greeley, she became a writer for the New York *Daily-Tribune*. During the time spent in New York, she not only broke the taboo against women as newspaper reporters, but she published *Woman in the Nineteenth Century* (1845), scandalizing the public with her revolutionary perspectives on the relationships between men and women. Her plea for equality was thrust upon a society so far removed from such a concept that wife-beating was being upheld in the courts at the time, and the ownership of property by women was three years away from achieving legal status in trend-setting New York State. Indeed, James Fenimore Cooper's last novel, *The Ways of the Hour* (1850), was largely a polemical howl of outrage against the passage of this law that had been debated for twelve years in the New York State Legislature. Against such a cultural background Margaret Fuller expanded upon an essay she had written in the July 1843 issue of *The Dial*, entitled "The Great Lawsuit: Man *versus* Men; Woman *versus* Women," and shaped it into *Woman in the Nineteenth Century*, the first American book defining the place of women in society, and offering a coherent alternative to their position.

This book, of course, did not come from a political or social vacuum. The rights of women were being debated in legislative chambers; Eliza Farnham and Lydia Maria Child, as well

as others, had written about legal inequities regarding women;
Lucretia Mott and Elizabeth Cady Stanton were doing work
that would culminate in the Seneca Falls Convention (1848);
and much other activity was going on in the field of women's
rights. But no statement addressed the controversy in the con-
text of its day as fully and as articulately as Margaret Fuller's
Woman in the Nineteenth Century did. Urged on by those
who had read and understood the implications of her original
article on the subject in *The Dial*, Margaret Fuller introduced
to America the genre of women's liberation books.

Her theoretical exploration of the relationships between the
sexes did not, however, guarantee her own fulfillment as a
woman. While working for Greeley, she had a bitter love affair
with an immigrant businessman named James Nathan. Much
of the record of what happened between Margaret Fuller and
James Nathan is still intact, since Nathan refused to return
her love letters, and they were subsequently published in a
volume entitled *Love-Letters of Margaret Fuller* (1903), with
an introduction by Julia Ward Howe. Her extreme confidence
notwithstanding, Margaret Fuller's sensitivity and passion made
her extremely vulnerable to James Nathan's cavalier treatment,
and there is no doubt she was hurt. Not surprisingly, she
seized an opportunity to go to Europe, traveling abroad as a
correspondent for the *Tribune*. She never returned to America.

Arriving in Europe in 1846, she discovered that *Woman in
the Nineteenth Century* had given her a degree of fame. Partly
as a consequence of her newly acquired reputation she met,
among others, George Sand, the Brownings, Carlyle, and, most
importantly, the Italian patriot Mazzini. Through him she
came to appreciate fully the cause of Italian independence.
Ultimately, she went to Italy and there met an Italian Marquis,
Giovanni Angelo Ossoli. Ignoring objections that the young
count was not intellectually worthy of her, she took him for a
lover and at the same time attracted him from his conservative
heritage into the midst of Italian revolutionary politics.

Although they were eventually married, their relationship
had to be kept secret for political and religious reasons. Margaret Fuller sequestered herself in a country village, where
she gave birth to a child, and subsequently returned to Rome,

Ossoli, and revolutionary politics. At the same time, she was sending dispatches to the *Tribune* and preparing a comprehensive history of the Italian Revolution. Although promising to be successful at first, the Revolution began to collapse when foreign troops intervened to restore papal authority. During the bitter seige of Rome, Margaret Fuller ignored the bombardment in order to nurse the sick and dying defenders of the city. She did so until French troops overcame Italian resistance, and on of all days, July 4, 1849, Rome fell. It was an irony that Margaret Fuller bitterly noted. With the Revolution crushed, there was little left for her to do other than return to America with Ossoli. What her reception at home would have been, what was contained in her history of the Revolution, the work which she regarded as her finest literary achievement, will never be known. Within sight of America, the ship broke up in a storm. Apparently refusing an opportunity to escape in a lifeboat without Ossoli, she lost her life, as did her child and her husband. The history of the Revolution was likewise lost.

Both her intellect and her passion are, however, to be found in her greatest extant literary work, *Woman in the Nineteenth Century*. The book is both an inner exploration of Margaret Fuller's personal quest for self-fulfillment and the first American extended polemical statement defining and advocating women's rights. Her personal quest was nothing less than a mystical one. Set against this tendency, however, was a full awareness of the worldly injustices confronting women. The struggle to seek abstract spiritual solutions in a world of everyday injustices was a problem not peculiar to Margaret Fuller. Emerson himself is a supreme example of an individual seeking non-tangible solutions in a world that resisted conforming to "transcendental" assumptions. Emerson's theories were put to their severest test over the issue of slavery. Margaret Fuller had her most direct confrontation by the barricades in Rome. The conflict between the two worlds that vied to possess her is manifested in *Woman in the Nineteenth Century*, the first American book to recognize that the liberation of women and the liberation of men are the same cause.

Although numerous editions of *Woman in the Nineteenth*

Century have appeared since the work was first published, all of them are based on the same text. The differences among them are in the varying collections of essays, extracts from journals and letters, and memoirs of Margaret Fuller that are appended to the basic work. The present text is the 1855 edition, including the preface by Arthur B. Fuller, the introduction by Horace Greeley, and the appendix by Margaret Fuller. This appendix is important both in its content and in its demonstration of Margaret Fuller's exhaustive efforts at bolstering her case.

The only editorial correction in the text is the inclusion on page 100 of a reference to Appendix G, rectifying an omission in the 1855 and subsequent editions.

The complete works of Margaret Fuller remain uncollected and unedited. Partial collections of Margaret Fuller's writings appear in Perry Miller's *Margaret Fuller: American Romantic* (New York, 1963), and Mason Wade's *The Writings of Margaret Fuller* (New York, 1941). Her major works include *Summer on the Lakes* (1844), *Papers on Literature and Art* (1846), and two posthumous books, *At Home and Abroad* (1856) and *Life Without and Life Within* (1859). While all these works are difficult to obtain, among her least accessible and most interesting literary efforts are those essays that appeared in *The Dial*. As to Margaret Fuller herself, numerous works have appeared about her, although as James Freeman Clarke wrote in 1883, "Margaret had so many aspects to her soul that she might furnish material for a hundred biographers, not all could be said even then." Some have, however, said it better than others. Perry Miller's introduction to *Margaret Fuller: American Romantic* is excellent. The best full length studies of her are Arthur W. Brown's *Margaret Fuller* (New York, 1964) and Mason Wade's *Margaret Fuller: Whetstone of Genius* (New York, 1940). Of special interest also is Joseph Deiss' *The Roman Years of Margaret Fuller* (New York, 1969).

BERNARD ROSENTHAL

State University of New York at Binghamton
July 5, 1971

WOMAN IN THE
NINETEENTH CENTURY

WOMAN

IN THE

NINETEENTH CENTURY

AND

KINDRED PAPERS

RELATING TO THE

Sphere, Condition and Duties, of Woman.

BY

MARGARET FULLER OSSOLI.

EDITED BY HER BROTHER,

ARTHUR B. FULLER.

WITH AN INTRODUCTION BY HORACE GREELEY.

———◆———

BOSTON:
PUBLISHED BY JOHN P. JEWETT & COMPANY.
CLEVELAND, OHIO:
JEWETT, PROCTOR & WORTHINGTON.
NEW YORK: SHELDON, LAMPORT & CO.
1855.

PREFACE.

It has been thought desirable that such papers of Margaret Fuller Ossoli as pertained to the condition, sphere and duties of Woman, should be collected and published together. The present volume contains not only her " Woman in the Nineteenth Century,"—which has been before published, but for some years out of print, and inaccessible to readers who have sought it,—but also several other papers, which have appeared at various times in the *Tribune* and elsewhere, and yet more which have never till now been published.

My free access to her private manuscripts has given to me many papers, relating to Woman, never intended for publication, which yet seem needful to this volume, in order to present a complete and harmonious view of her thoughts on this important theme. I have preferred to publish them without alteration, as most just to her views and to the reader ; though, doubtless, she would have varied their expression and form before giving them to the press.

It seems right here to remark, in order to avoid any misapprehension, that Margaret Ossoli's thoughts were not directed so exclusively to the subject of the present volume as have been the minds of some others. As to the movement for the emancipation of Woman from the unjust burdens and disabilities to which she has been subject even in our own land, my sister could neither remain indifferent nor silent ; yet she preferred, as in respect to every other reform, to act independently and to speak independently from her own stand-point, and never to merge her individuality in any existing organization. This she did, not as condemning such organizations, nor yet as judging them wholly unwise or uncalled for, but because she believed she could herself accomplish more for their true and high objects, unfettered by such organizations, than if a member of them. The opinions avowed throughout this volume, and wherever expressed, will, then, be found, whether consonant with the reader's or no, in all cases honestly and heartily her own,— the result of her own thought and faith. She never speaks, never did speak, for any clique or sect, but as her individual judgment, her reason and conscience, her observation and experience, taught her to speak.

I could have wished that some one other than a brother should have spoken a few fitting words of Margaret Fuller, as a woman, to form a brief but proper accompaniment to this volume, which may reach some who have never read her "Memoirs," recently published, or have never known her in personal life. This seemed the more desirable, because the strictest verity in speaking of her must seem, to such as knew her not, to be eulogy. But, after several disappointments as to the editorship of the volume, the duty, at last, has seemed to devolve upon me ; and I have no reason to shrink from it but a sense of inadequacy.

It is often supposed that literary women, and those who are active and earnest in promoting great intellectual, philanthropic, or religious movements, must of necessity neglect the domestic concerns of life. It may be that this is sometimes so, nor can such neglect be too severely reprehended ; yet this is by no means a necessary result. Some of the most devoted mothers the world has ever known, and whose homes were the abode of every domestic virtue, themselves the embodiment of all these, have been women whose minds were highly cultured, who loved and devoted both thought and time to literature, and were active in philanthropic and diffusive efforts for the welfare of the race.

The letter to M., which is published on page 345, is inserted chiefly as showing the integrity and wisdom with which Margaret advised her friends ; the frankness with which she pointed out to every young woman who asked counsel any deficiencies of character, and the duties of life ; and that among these latter she gave due place to the humblest which serve to make home attractive and happy. It is but simple justice for me to bear, in conjunction with many others, my tribute to her domestic virtues and fidelity to all home duties. That her mind found chief delight in the lowest forms of these duties may not be true, and it would be sad if it were ; but it is strictly true that none, however humble, were either slighted or shunned.

In common with a younger sister and brother, I shared her care in my early instruction, and found ever one of the truest counsellors in a sister who scorned not the youngest mind nor the simplest intellectual wants in her love for communion, through converse or the silent page, with the minds of the greatest and most gifted.

During a lingering illness, in childhood, well do I remember her as the angel of the sick-chamber, reading much to me from books useful and appropriate, and telling many a narrative not only fitted to wile away the pain of disease and the weariness of long confinement, but to elevate the mind and heart, and to direct them to all things noble and holy ; ever ready to watch while I slept, and to perform every gentle and kindly office. But her care of the sick — that she did not neglect, but was eminent in that sphere of womanly duty, even when no tie of kindred claimed this of her, Mr. Cass's letter abundantly shows ; and also that this gentleness was united to a heroism which most call manly, but which, I believe, may as justly be called truly womanly. Mr. Cass's letter is inserted because it arrived too late to find a place in her " Memoirs," and yet more because it bears much on Margaret Ossoli's characteristics as a woman.

A few also of her private letters and papers, not bearing, save, indirectly, on the subject of this volume, are yet inserted in it, as further illustrative of her thought, feeling and action, in life's various relations. It is believed that nothing which exhibits a true woman, especially in her relations to others as friend, sister, daughter, wife, or mother, can fail to interest and be of value to her sex, indeed to all who are interested in human welfare and advancement, since these latter so much depend on the fidelity of Woman. Nor will anything pertaining to the education and care of children be deemed irrelevant, especially by mothers, upon whom these duties must always largely devolve.

Of the intellectual gifts and wide culture of Margaret Fuller there is no need that I should speak, nor is it wise that one standing in my relation to her should. Those who knew her personally feel that no words ever flowed from her pen equalling the eloquent utterances of her lips ; yet her works, though not always a clear expression of her thoughts, are the evidences to which the world will look as proof of her mental greatness.

On one point, however, I do wish to bear testimony — not needed with those who knew her well, but interesting, perhaps, to some readers into whose hands this volume may fall. It is on a subject which one who knew her from his childhood up — at *home*, where best the *heart* and *soul* can be known, — in the unrestrained hours of domestic life, — in various scenes, and not for a few days, nor under any peculiar circumstances — can speak with confidence, because he speaks what he " doth know, and testifieth what he hath seen." It relates to her Christian faith and hope. " With all her intellectual gifts, with all her high, moral, and noble characteristics," there are some who will ask, " was her intellectual power sanctified by Christian faith as its basis? Were her moral qualities, her beneficent life, the results of a renewed heart ? " I feel no hesitation here, nor would think it worth while to answer such questions at all, were her life to be read and known by all who read this volume, and were I not influenced also, in some degree, by the tone which has characterized a few sectarian reviews of her works, chiefly in foreign periodicals. Surely, if the Saviour's test, " By their fruits ye shall know them," be the true one, Margaret Ossoli was pre-eminently a Christian. If a life of constant self-sacrifice, — if devotion to the welfare of kindred and the race, — if conformity to what she believed God's law, so that her life seemed ever the truest form of prayer, active obedience to the Deity, — in fine, if carrying Christianity into all the departments of action, so far as human infirmity allows, — if these be the proofs of a Christian, then whoever has read her " Memoirs " thoughtfully, and without sectarian prejudice or the use of sectarian standards of judgment, must feel her to have been a Christian. But not alone in outward life, in mind and heart, too, was she a Christian. The being brought into frequent and intimate contact with religious persons has been one of the chief privileges of my vocation, but never yet have I met with any person whose reverence for holy things was deeper than hers. Abhorring, as all honest minds must, every species of cant, she respected true religious thought and feeling, by whomsoever cherished. God seemed nearer to her than to any person I have ever known. In the influences of His Holy Spirit upon the heart she fully believed, and in experience realized them. Jesus, the friend of man, can never have been more truly loved and honored than she loved and honored him. I am aware that this is strong language, but strength of language cannot equal the strength of my conviction on a point where I have had the best opportunities of judgment. Rich as is the religion of Jesus in its list of holy confessors, yet it can spare and would exclude none who in heart, mind and life, confessed and reverenced him as did she. Among my earliest recollections, is her devoting much time to a thorough examination of the evidences of Christianity, and ultimately declaring that to her, better than all arguments or usual processes of proof, was the soul's want of a divine religion, and the voice within that soul which declared the teachings of Christ to be true and from God ; and one of my most cherished possessions is that Bible which she so diligently and thoughtfully read, and which bears, in her own handwriting, so many proofs of discriminating and prayerful perusal. As in regard to reformatory movements so here, she joined no organized body of believers, sympathizing with all of them whose views were noble and Christian ; deploring and bearing faithful testimony against anything she deemed narrowness or perversion in theology or life.

This volume from her hand is now before the reader. The fact that a large share of it was never written or revised by its authoress for publication will be kept in view, as explaining any inaccuracy of expression or repetition of thought, should such occur in its pages. Nor will it be deemed surprising, if, in papers written by so progressive a person, at so various periods of life, and under widely-varied circumstances, there should not always be found perfect unison as to every expressed opinion.

It is probable that this will soon be followed by another volume, containing a republication of " Summer on the Lakes," and also the " Letters from Europe," by the same hand.

In the preparation of this volume much valuable assistance has been afforded by Mr. Greeley, of the New York *Tribune*, who has been earnest in his desire and efforts for the diffusion of what Margaret has written.

A. B. F.

BOSTON, *May* 10*th*, 1855.

INTRODUCTION.

THE problem of Woman's position, or " sphere," — of her duties, responsibilities, rights and immunities *as* Woman, — fitly
attracts a large and still-increasing measure of attention from the
thinkers and agitators of our time. The legislators, so called, —
those who ultimately enact into statutes what the really govern-
ing class (to wit, the thinkers) have originated, matured and
gradually commended to the popular comprehension and acceptance, — are not as yet much occupied with this problem, only fit-
fully worried and more or less consciously puzzled by it. More
commonly they merely echo the mob's shallow retort to the pe-
tition of any strong-minded daughter or sister, who demands
that she be allowed a voice in disposing of the money wrenched
from her hard earnings by inexorable taxation, or in shaping the
laws by which she is ruled, judged, and is liable to be sentenced
to prison or to death, " It is a woman's business to obey her husband, keep his home tidy, and nourish and train his children."
But when she rejoins to this, " Very true ; but suppose I choose
not to have a husband, or am not chosen for a wife — what then ?
I am still subject to your laws. Why am I not entitled, as a
rational human being, to a voice in shaping them ? I have physical needs, and must somehow earn a living. Why should I not
be at liberty to earn it in any honest and useful calling ? " — the
mob's flout is hushed, and the legislator is struck dumb also.
They were already at the end of their scanty resources of logic, and
it would be cruel for woman to ask further : " Suppose me a wife,
and my husband a drunken prodigal — what am I to do then ?
May I not earn food for my babes without being exposed to have
it snatched from their mouths to replenish the rumseller's till, and

aggravate my husband's madness? If some sympathizing relative sees fit to leave me a bequest wherewith to keep my little ones together, why may I not be legally enabled to secure this to their use and benefit? In short, why am I not regarded by the law as a *soul*, responsible for my acts to God and humanity, and not as a mere body, devoted to the unreasoning service of my husband?" The state gives no answer, and the champions of her policy evince wisdom in imitating her silence.

The writer of the following pages was one of the earliest as well as ablest among American women, to demand for her sex equality before the law with her titular lord and master. Her writings on this subject have the force which springs from the ripening of profound reflection into assured conviction. She wrote as one who had observed, and who deeply felt what she deliberately uttered. Others have since spoken more fluently, more variously, with a greater affluence of illustration; but none, it is believed, more earnestly or more forcibly. It is due to her memory, as well as to the great and living cause of which she was so eminent and so fearless an advocate, that what she thought and said with regard to the position of her sex and its limitations, should be fully and fairly placed before the public. For several years past her principal essay on "Woman," here given, has not been purchasable at any price, and has only with great difficulty been accessible to the general reader. To place it within the reach of those who need and require it, is the main impulse to the publication of this volume; but the accompanying essays and papers will be found equally worthy of thoughtful consideration.

H. GREELEY.

PREFACE

WOMAN IN THE NINETEENTH CENTURY.

THE following essay is a reproduction, modified and expanded,
of an article published in "The Dial, Boston, July, 1843," under
the title of "The Great Lawsuit. — Man *versus* Men ; Woman
versus Women."

This article excited a good deal of sympathy, and still more
interest. It is in compliance with wishes expressed from many
quarters that it is prepared for publication in its present form.

Objections having been made to the former title, as not sufficiently easy to be understood, the present has been substituted as
expressive of the main purpose of the essay ; though, by myself,
the other is preferred, partly for the reason others do not
like it,— that is, that it requires some thought to see what it
means, and might thus prepare the reader to meet me on my own
ground. Besides, it offers a larger scope, and is, in that way,
more just to my desire. I meant by that title to intimate the
fact that, while it is the destiny of Man, in the course of the ages,
to ascertain and fulfil the law of his being, so that his life shall
be seen, as a whole, to be that of an angel or messenger, the
action of prejudices and passions which attend, in the day, the
growth of the individual, is continually obstructing the holy work
that is to make the earth a part of heaven. By Man I mean
both man and woman ; these are the two halves of one thought.
I lay no especial stress on the welfare of either. I believe that
the development of the one cannot be effected without that of the
other. My highest wish is that this truth should be distinctly
and rationally apprehended, and the conditions of life and free-

dom recognized as the same for the daughters and the sons of time ; twin exponents of a divine thought.

I solicit a sincere and patient attention from those who open the following pages at all. I solicit of women that they will lay it to heart to ascertain what is for them the liberty of law. It is for this, and not for any, the largest, extension of partial privileges that I seek. I ask them, if interested by these suggestions, to search their own experience and intuitions for better, and fill up with fit materials the trenches that hedge them in. From men I ask a noble and earnest attention to anything that can be offered on this great and still obscure subject, such as I have met from many with whom I stand in private relations.

And may truth, unpolluted by prejudice, vanity or selfishness, be granted daily more and more as the due of inheritance, and only valuable conquest for us all !

November, 1844.

WOMAN

IN THE

NINETEENTH CENTURY.

" Frailty, thy name is WOMAN."
" The Earth waits for her Queen."

THE connection between these quotations may not be
obvious, but it is strict. Yet would any contradict us,
if we made them applicable to the other side, and began
also,

> Frailty, thy name is MAN.
> The Earth waits for its King?

Yet Man, if not yet fully installed in his powers, has
given much earnest of his claims. Frail he is indeed,—
how frail! how impure! Yet often has the vein of gold
displayed itself amid the baser ores, and Man has appeared before us in princely promise worthy of his future.

If, oftentimes, we see the prodigal son feeding on the
husks in the fair field no more his own, anon we raise
the eyelids, heavy from bitter tears, to behold in him the
radiant apparition of genius and love, demanding not
less than the all of goodness, power and beauty. We
see that in him the largest claim finds a due foundation.

That claim is for no partial sway, no exclusive possession. He cannot be satisfied with any one gift of life, any one department of knowledge or telescopic peep at the heavens. He feels himself called to understand and aid Nature, that she may, through his intelligence, be raised and interpreted; to be a student of, and servant to, the universe-spirit; and king of his planet, that, as an angelic minister, he may bring it into conscious harmony with the law of that spirit.

In clear, triumphant moments, many times, has rung through the spheres the prophecy of his jubilee; and those moments, though past in time, have been translated into eternity by thought; the bright signs they left hang in the heavens, as single stars or constellations, and, already, a thickly sown radiance consoles the wanderer in the darkest night. Other heroes since Hercules have fulfilled the zodiac of beneficent labors, and then given up their mortal part to the fire without a murmur; while no God dared deny that they should have their reward,

> Siquis tamen, Hercule, siquis
> Forte Deo doliturus erit, data præmia nollet,
> Sed meruise dari sciet, invitus que probabit,
> Assensere Dei.

Sages and lawgivers have bent their whole nature to the search for truth, and thought themselves happy if they could buy, with the sacrifice of all temporal ease and pleasure, one seed for the future Eden. Poets and priests have strung the lyre with the heart-strings, poured out their best blood upon the altar, which, reared anew from age to age, shall at last sustain the flame pure enough to rise to highest heaven. Shall we not name with as deep a benediction those who, if not so immediately, or so consciously, in connection with the eternal truth, yet, led and fashioned by a divine instinct, serve no less to develop and interpret the open secret of love passing into life, energy creating for the purpose of happiness; the artist whose hand, drawn by a preëxistent harmony to a certain medium, moulds it to forms of life more highly and completely organized than are seen elsewhere, and, by carrying out the intention of nature, reveals her meaning to those who are not yet wise enough to divine it; the philosopher who listens steadily for laws and causes, and from those obvious infers those yet unknown; the historian who, in faith that all events must have their reason and their aim, records them, and thus fills archives from which the youth of prophets may be fed; the man of science dissecting the statements, testing the facts and demonstrating order, even where he cannot its purpose?

Lives, too, which bear none of these names, have yielded tones of no less significance. The candlestick set in a low place has given light as faithfully, where it was needed, as that upon the hill. In close alleys, in dismal nooks, the Word has been read as distinctly, as when shown by angels to holy men in the dark prison. Those who till a spot of earth scarcely larger than is wanted for a grave, have deserved that the sun should shine upon its sod till violets answer.

So great has been, from time to time, the promise,

that, in all ages, men have said the gods themselves came down to dwell with them; that the All-Creating wandered on the earth to taste, in a limited nature, the sweetness of virtue; that the All-Sustaining incarnated himself to guard, in space and time, the destinies of this world; that heavenly genius dwelt among the shepherds, to sing to them and teach them how to sing. Indeed,

" Der stets den Hirten gnadig sich bewies."

"He has constantly shown himself favorable to shepherds."

And the dwellers in green pastures and natural students of the stars were selected to hail, first among men, the holy child, whose life and death were to present the type of excellence, which has sustained the heart of so large a portion of mankind in these later generations.

Such marks have been made by the footsteps of *man* (still, alas! to be spoken of as the *ideal* man), wherever he has passed through the wilderness of *men*, and whenever the pigmies stepped in one of those, they felt dilate within the breast somewhat that promised nobler stature and purer blood. They were impelled to forsake their evil ways of decrepit scepticism and covetousness of corruptible possessions. Convictions flowed in upon them. They, too, raised the cry: God is living, now, to-day; and all beings are brothers, for they are his children. Simple words enough, yet which only angelic natures can use or hear in their full, free sense.

These were the triumphant moments; but soon the lower nature took its turn, and the era of a truly human life was postponed.

Thus is man still a stranger to his inheritance, still a pleader, still a pilgrim. Yet his happiness is secure in the end. And now, no more a glimmering consciousness, but assurance begins to be felt and spoken, that the highest ideal Man can form of his own powers is that which he is destined to attain. Whatever the soul knows how to seek, it cannot fail to obtain. This is the Law and the Prophets. Knock and it shall be opened; seek and ye shall find. It is demonstrated; it is a maxim. Man no longer paints his proper nature in some form, and says, " Prometheus had it; it is God-like; " but " Man must have it; it is human." However disputed by many, however ignorantly used, or falsified by those who do receive it, the fact of an universal, unceasing revelation has been too clearly stated in words to be lost sight of in thought; and sermons preached from the text, " Be ye perfect," are the only sermons of a pervasive and deep-searching influence.

But, among those who meditate upon this text, there is a great difference of view as to the way in which perfection shall be sought.

" Through the intellect," say some. " Gather from every growth of life its seed of thought; look behind every symbol for its law; if thou canst *see* clearly, the rest will follow."

" Through the life," say others. " Do the best thou knowest to-day. Shrink not from frequent error in this gradual, fragmentary state. Follow thy light for as much as it will show thee; be faithful as far as thou canst, in hope that faith presently will lead to sight. Help others, without blaming their need of thy help. Love much, and be forgiven."

" It needs not intellect, needs not experience," says a third. " If you took the true way, your destiny would be accomplished in a purer and more natural order. You would not learn through facts of thought or action, but express through them the certainties of wisdom. In quietness yield thy soul to the causal soul. Do not disturb thy apprenticeship by premature effort; neither check the tide of instruction by methods of thy own. Be still; seek not, but wait in obedience. Thy commission will be given."

Could we indeed say what we want, could we give a description of the child that is lost, he would be found. As soon as the soul can affirm clearly that a certain demonstration is wanted, it is at hand. When the Jewish prophet described the Lamb, as the expression of what was required by the coming era, the time drew nigh. But we say not, see not as yet, clearly, what we would. Those who call for a more triumphant expression of love, a love that cannot be crucified, show not a perfect sense of what has already been given. Love has already been expressed, that made all things new, that gave the worm its place and ministry as well as the eagle; a love to which it was alike to descend into the depths of hell, or to sit at the right hand of the Father.

Yet, no doubt, a new manifestation is at hand, a new hour in the day of Man. We cannot expect to see any one sample of completed being, when the mass of men still lie engaged in the sod, or use the freedom of their limbs only with wolfish energy. The tree cannot come to flower till its root be free from the cankering worm, and its whole growth open to air and light. While any one is base, none can be entirely free and noble. Yet something new shall presently be shown of the life of man, for hearts crave, if minds do not know how to ask it.

Among the strains of prophecy, the following, by an earnest mind of a foreign land, written some thirty years ago, is not yet outgrown ; and it has the merit of being a positive appeal from the heart, instead of a critical declaration what Man should *not* do.

" The ministry of Man implies that he must be filled from the divine fountains which are being engendered through all eternity, so that, at the mere name of his master, he may be able to cast all his enemies into the abyss ; that he may deliver all parts of nature from the barriers that imprison them ; that he may purge the terrestrial atmosphere from the poisons that infect it ; that he may preserve the bodies of men from the corrupt influences that surround, and the maladies that afflict them ; still more, that he may keep their souls pure from the malignant insinuations which pollute, and the gloomy images that obscure them ; that he may restore its serenity to the Word, which false words of men fill with mourning and sadness ; that he may satisfy the desires of the angels, who await from him the development of the marvels of nature ; that, in fine, his world may be filled with God, as eternity is."*

Another attempt we will give, by an obscure observer

* St. Martin.

of our own day and country, to draw some lines of the desired image. It was suggested by seeing the design of Crawford's Orpheus, and connecting with the circumstance of the American, in his garret at Rome, making choice of this subject, that of Americans here at home showing such ambition to represent the character, by calling their prose and verse " Orphic sayings " — " Orphics." We wish we could add that they have shown that musical apprehension of the progress of Nature through her ascending gradations which entitled them so to do, but their attempts are frigid, though sometimes grand; in their strain we are not warmed by the fire which fertilized the soil of Greece.

Orpheus was a lawgiver by theocratic commission. He understood nature, and made her forms move to his music. He told her secrets in the form of hymns, Nature as seen in the mind of God. His soul went forth toward all beings, yet could remain sternly faithful to a chosen type of excellence. Seeking what he loved, he feared not death nor hell; neither could any shape of dread daunt his faith in the power of the celestial harmony that filled his soul.

It seemed significant of the state of things in this country, that the sculptor should have represented the seer at the moment when he was obliged with his hand to shade his eyes.

> Each Orpheus must to the depths descend ;
> For only thus the Poet can be wise ;
> Must make the sad Persephone his friend,
> And buried love to second life arise ;

Again his love must lose through too much love,
Must lose his life by living life too true,
For what he sought below is passed above,
Already done is all that he would do ;
Must tune all being with his single lyre,
Must melt all rocks free from their primal pain,
Must search all nature with his one soul's fire,
Must bind anew all forms in heavenly chain.
If he already sees what he must do,
Well may he shade his eyes from the far-shining view.

A better comment could not be made on what is required to perfect Man, and place him in that superior position for which he was designed, than by the interpretation of Bacon upon the legends of the Syren coast. "When the wise Ulysses passed," says he, " he caused his mariners to stop their ears with wax, knowing there was in them no power to resist the lure of that voluptuous song. But he, the much experienced man, who wished to be experienced in all, and use all to the service of wisdom, desired to hear the song that he might understand its meaning. Yet, distrusting his own power to be firm in his better purpose, hé caused himself to be bound to the mast, that he might be kept secure against his own weakness. But Orpheus passed unfettered, so absorbed in singing hymns to the gods that he could not even hear those sounds of degrading enchantment."

Meanwhile, not a few believe, and men themselves have expressed the opinion, that the time is come when Eurydice is to call for an Orpheus, rather than Orpheus for Eurydice; that the idea of Man, however imperfectly brought out, has been far more so than that of Woman;

that she, the other half of the same thought, the other chamber of the heart of life, needs now take her turn in the full pulsation, and that improvement in the daughters will best aid in the reformation of the sons of this age.

It should be remarked that, as the principle of liberty is better understood, and more nobly interpreted, a broader protest is made in behalf of Woman. As men become aware that few men have had a fair chance, they are inclined to say that no women have had a fair chance. The French Revolution, that strangely disguised angel, bore witness in favor of Woman, but interpreted her claims no less ignorantly than those of Man. Its idea of happiness did not rise beyond outward enjoyment, unobstructed by the tyranny of others. The title it gave was "citoyen," "citoyenne;" and it is not unimportant to Woman that even this species of equality was awarded her. Before, she could be condemned to perish on the scaffold for treason, not as a citizen, but as a subject. The right with which this title then invested a human being was that of bloodshed and license. The Goddess of Liberty was impure. As we read the poem addressed to her, not long since, by Beranger, we can scarcely refrain from tears as painful as the tears of blood that flowed when "such crimes were committed in her name." Yes! Man, born to purify and animate the unintelligent and the cold, can, in his madness, degrade and pollute no less the fair and the chaste. Yet truth was prophesied in the ravings of that hideous fever, caused by long ignorance and abuse. Europe is conning a valued lesson from the blood-stained page. The same tendencies, further unfolded, will bear good fruit in this country.

Yet, by men in this country, as by the Jews, when Moses was leading them to the promised land, everything has been done that inherited depravity could do, to hinder the promise of Heaven from its fulfilment. The cross, here as elsewhere, has been planted only to be blasphemed by cruelty and fraud. The name of the Prince of Peace has been profaned by all kinds of injustice toward the Gentile whom he said he came to save. But I need not speak of what has been done towards the Red Man, the Black Man. Those deeds are the scoff of the world ; and they have been accompanied by such pious words that the gentlest would not dare to intercede with " Father, forgive them, for they know not what they do."

Here, as elsewhere, the gain of creation consists always in the growth of individual minds, which live and aspire, as flowers bloom and birds sing, in the midst of morasses; and in the continual development of that thought, the thought of human destiny, which is given to eternity adequately to express, and which ages of failure only seemingly impede. Only seemingly ; and whatever seems to the contrary, this country is as surely destined to elucidate a great moral law, as Europe was to promote the mental culture of Man.

Though the national independence be blurred by the servility of individuals ; though freedom and equality have been proclaimed only to leave room for a monstrous display of slave-dealing and slave-keeping ; though the free American so often feels himself free, like the Roman, only to pamper his appetites and his indolence through the misery of his fellow-beings ; still it is not in vain that the verbal statement has been made, "All men are born free and equal." There it stands, a golden certainty wherewith to encourage the good, to shame the bad. The New World may be called clearly to perceive that it incurs the utmost penalty if it reject or oppress the sorrowful brother. And, if men are deaf, the angels hear. But men cannot be deaf. It is inevitable that an external freedom, an independence of the encroachments of other men, such as has been achieved for the nation, should be so also for every member of it. That which has once been clearly conceived in the intelligence cannot fail, sooner or later, to be acted out. It has become a law as irrevocable as that of the Medes in their ancient dominion ; men will privately sin against it, but the law, as expressed by a leading mind of the age,

> "Tutti fatti a sembianza d'un Solo,
>   Figli tutti d'un solo riscatto,
>   In qual'ora, in qual parte del suolo
>   Trascorriamo quest' aura vital,
>   Siam fratelli, siam stretti ad un patto :
>   Maladetto colui che lo infrange,
>   Che s'innalza sul fiacco che piange
>   Che contrista uno spirto immortal." *

> "All made in the likeness of the One,
>   All children of one ransom,
> In whatever hour, in whatever part of the soil,
>   We draw this vital air,

* Manzoni.

> We are brothers ; we must be bound by one compact ;
>   Accursed he who infringes it,
> Who raises himself upon the weak who weep,
>   Who saddens an immortal spirit.''

This law cannot fail of universal recognition. Accursed be he who willingly saddens an immortal spirit—doomed to infamy in later, wiser ages, doomed in future stages of his own being to deadly penance, only short of death. Accursed be he who sins in ignorance, if that ignorance be caused by sloth.

We sicken no less at the pomp than the strife of words. We feel that never were lungs so puffed with the wind of declamation, on moral and religious subjects, as now. We are tempted to implore these "word-heroes," these word-Catos, word-Christs, to beware of cant* above all things; to remember that hypocrisy is the most hopeless as well as the meanest of crimes, and that those must surely be polluted by it, who do not reserve a part of their morality and religion for private use. Landor says that he cannot have a great deal of mind who cannot afford to let the larger part of it lie fallow; and what is true of genius is not less so of virtue. The tongue is a valuable member, but should appropriate but a small part of the vital juices that are needful all over the body. We feel that the mind may

---

* Dr. Johnson's one piece of advice should be written on every door : " Clear your mind of cant.'' But Byron, to whom it was so acceptable, in clearing away the noxious vine, shook down the building. Sterling's emendation is worthy of honor :

" Realize your cant, not cast it off.''

"grow black and rancid in the smoke" even "of altars."
We start up from the harangue to go into our closet and
shut the door.   There inquires the spirit, "Is this rhetoric the bloom of healthy blood, or a false pigment art-
fully laid on?"   And yet again we know where is so
much smoke, must be some fire; with so much talk about
virtue and freedom, must be mingled some desire for
them; that it cannot be in vain that such have become
the common topics of conversation among men, rather than
schemes for tyranny and plunder, that the very newspapers see it best to proclaim themselves "Pilgrims,"
"Puritans," "Heralds of Holiness."   The king that
maintains so costly a retinue cannot be a mere boast, or
Carabbas fiction.   We have waited here long in the dust;
we are tired and hungry; but the triumphal procession
must appear at last.

Of all its banners, none has been more steadily upheld, and under none have more valor and willingness for
real sacrifices been shown, than that of the champions
of the enslaved African.   And this band it is, which,
partly from a natural following out of principles, partly
because many women have been prominent in that cause,
makes, just now, the warmest appeal in behalf of Woman.

Though there has been a growing liberality on this
subject, yet society at large is not so prepared for the
demands of this party, but that its members are, and will
be for some time, coldly regarded as the Jacobins of their
day.

"Is it not enough," cries the irritated trader, "that
you have done all you could to break up the national

union, and thus destroy the prosperity of our country, but now you must be trying to break up family union, to take my wife away from the cradle and the kitchen-hearth to vote at polls, and preach from a pulpit? Of course, if she does such things, she cannot attend to those of her own sphere. She is happy enough as she is. She has more leisure than I have,— every means of improvement, every indulgence."

" Have you asked her whether she was satisfied with these *indulgences ?* "

" No, but I know she is. She is too amiable to desire what would make me unhappy, and too judicious to wish to step beyond the sphere of her sex. I will never consent to have our peace disturbed by any such discussions."

" ' Consent — you?' it is not consent from you that is in question — it is assent from your wife."

" Am not I the head of my house ? "

" You are not the head of your wife. God has given her a mind of her own."

" I am the head, and she the heart."

" God grant you play true to one another, then ! I suppose I am to be grateful that you did not say she was only the hand. If the head represses no natural pulse of the heart, there can be no question as to your giving your consent. Both will be of one accord, and there needs but to present any question to get a full and true answer. There is no need of precaution, of indulgence, nor consent. But our doubt is whether the heart *does* consent with the head, or only obeys its decrees with a passiveness that precludes the exercise of its natural powers, or a repugnance that turns sweet qualities to bitter, or a doubt that lays waste the fair occasions of life. It is to ascertain the truth that we propose some liberating measures."

Thus vaguely are these questions proposed and discussed at present. But their being proposed at all implies much thought, and suggests more. Many women are considering within themselves what they need that they have not, and what they can have if they find they need it. Many men are considering whether women are capable of being and having more than they are and have, *and* whether, if so, it will be best to consent to improvement in their condition.

This morning, I open the Boston " Daily Mail," and find in its " poet's corner " a translation of Schiller's " Dignity of Woman." In the advertisement of a book on America, I see in the table of contents this sequence, " Republican Institutions. American Slavery. American Ladies."

I open the " *Deutsche Schnellpost*," published in New York, and find at the head of a column, *Judenund Frauen-emancipation in Ungarn* — " Emancipation of Jews and Women in Hungary."

The past year has seen action in the Rhode Island legislature, to secure married women rights over their own property, where men showed that a very little examination of the subject could teach them much ; an article in the Democratic Review on the same subject more largely considered, written by a woman, impelled, it is said, by glaring wrong to a distinguished friend, hav-

ing shown the defects in the existing laws, and the state
of opinion from which they spring; and an answer from
the revered old man, J. Q. Adams, in some respects the
Phocion of his time, to an address made him by some
ladies. To this last I shall again advert in another place.

These symptoms of the times have come under my
view quite accidentally : one who seeks, may, each
month or week, collect more.

The numerous party, whose opinions are already
labeled and adjusted too much to their mind to admit
of any new light, strive, by lectures on some model-
woman of bride-like beauty and gentleness, by writing
and lending little treatises, intended to mark out with
precision the limits of Woman's sphere, and Woman's
mission, to prevent other than the rightful shepherd from
climbing the wall, or the flock from using any chance to
go astray.

Without enrolling ourselves at once on either side, let
us look upon the subject from the best point of view
which to-day offers ; no better, it is to be feared, than
a high house-top. A high hill-top, or at least a cathedral-
spire, would be desirable.

It may well be an Anti-Slavery party that pleads for
Woman, if we consider merely that she does not hold
property on equal terms with men; so that, if a husband
dies without making a will, the wife, instead of taking
at once his place as head of the family, inherits only a
part of his fortune, often brought him by herself, as if
she were a child, or ward only, not an equal partner.

We will not speak of the innumerable instances in

which profligate and idle men live upon the earnings of industrious wives ; or if the wives leave them, and take with them the children, to perform the double duty of mother and father, follow from place to place, and threaten to rob them of the children, if deprived of the rights of a husband, as they call them, planting themselves in their poor lodgings, frightening them into paying tribute by taking from them the children, running into debt at the expense of these otherwise so overtasked helots. Such instances count up by scores within my own memory. I have seen the husband who had stained himself by a long course of low vice, till his wife was wearied from her heroic forgiveness, by finding that his treachery made it useless, and that if she would provide bread for herself and her children, she must be separate from his ill fame — I have known this man come to install himself in the chamber of a woman who loathed him, and say she should never take food without his company. I have known these men steal their children, whom they knew they had no means to maintain, take them into dissolute company, expose them to bodily danger, to frighten the poor woman, to whom, it seems, the fact that she alone had borne the pangs of their birth, and nourished their infancy, does not give an equal right to them. I do believe that this mode of kidnapping — and it is frequent enough in all classes of society — will be by the next age viewed as it is by Heaven now, and that the man who avails himself of the shelter of men's laws to steal from a mother her own children, or arrogate any superior right in them, save that of superior virtue, will bear the stigma he deserves, in common with him who steals grown men from their mother-land, their hopes, and their homes.

I said, we will not speak of this now; yet I *have* spoken, for the subject makes me feel too much. I could give instances that would startle the most vulgar and callous ; but I will not, for the public opinion of their own sex is already against such men, and where cases of extreme tyranny are made known, there is private action in the wife's favor. But she ought not to need this, nor, I think, can she long. Men must soon see that as, on their own ground, Woman is the weaker party, she ought to have legal protection, which would make such oppression impossible. But I would not deal with "atrocious instances," except in the way of illustration, neither demand from men a partial redress in some one matter, but go to the root of the whole. If principles could be established, particulars would adjust themselves aright. Ascertain the true destiny of Woman; give her legitimate hopes, and a standard within herself; marriage and all other relations would by degrees be harmonized with these.

But to return to the historical progress of this matter. Knowing that there exists in the minds of men a tone of feeling toward women as toward slaves, such as is expressed in the common phrase, " Tell that to women and children ; " that the infinite soul can only work through them in already ascertained limits; that the gift of reason, Man's highest prerogative, is allotted to them in much lower degree ; that they must be kept from mischief and melancholy by being constantly engaged in active labor, which is to be furnished and directed by those better able to think, &c., &c.,— we need not multiply instances, for who can review the experience of last week without recalling words which imply, whether in jest or earnest, these views, or views like these,— knowing this, can we wonder that many reformers think that measures are not likely to be taken in behalf of women, unless their wishes could be publicly represented by women?

"That can never be necessary," cry the other side. "All men are privately influenced by women; each has his wife, sister, or female friends, and is too much biased by these relations to fail of representing their interests; and, if this is not enough, let them propose and enforce their wishes with the pen. The beauty of home would be destroyed, the delicacy of the sex be violated, the dignity of halls of legislation degraded, by an attempt to introduce them there. Such duties are inconsistent with those of a mother;" and then we have ludicrous pictures of ladies in hysterics at the polls, and senate-chambers filled with cradles.

But if, in reply, we admit as truth that Woman seems destined by nature rather for the inner circle, we must add that the arrangements of civilized life have not been, as yet, such as to secure it to her. Her circle, if the duller, is not the quieter. If kept from "excitement," she is not from drudgery. Not only the Indian squaw carries the burdens of the camp, but the favorites of **Louis XIV.** accompany him in his journeys, and the washerwoman stands at her tub, and carries home her work at all seasons, and in all states of health. Those who think the physical circumstances of Woman would make a part in the affairs of national government unsuitable, are by no means those who think it impossible for negresses to endure field-work, even during pregnancy, or for sempstresses to go through their killing labors.

As to the use of the pen, there was quite as much opposition to Woman's possessing herself of that help to free agency as there is now to her seizing on the rostrum or the desk; and she is likely to draw, from a permission to plead her cause that way, opposite inferences to what might be wished by those who now grant it.

As to the possibility of her filling with grace and dignity any such position, we should think those who had seen the great actresses, and heard the Quaker preachers of modern times, would not doubt that Woman can express publicly the fulness of thought and creation, without losing any of the peculiar beauty of her sex. What can pollute and tarnish is to act thus from any motive except that something needs to be said or done. Woman could take part in the processions, the songs, the dances of old religion; no one fancied her delicacy was impaired by appearing in public for such a cause.

As to her home, she is not likely to leave it more than she now does for balls, theatres, meetings for promoting missions, revival meetings, and others to which she flies, in hope of an animation for her existence commensurate with what she sees enjoyed by men. Governors of ladies'-fairs are no less engrossed by such a charge, than the governor of a state by his; presidents of Washingtonian societies no less away from home than presidents of conventions. If men look straitly to it, they will find that, unless their lives are domestic, those ot the women will not be. A house is no home unless it contain food and fire for the mind as well as for the body. The female Greek, of our day, is as much in the street as the male to cry, "What news?" We doubt not it was the same in Athens of old. The women, shut out from the market-place, made up for it at the religious festivals. For human beings are not so constituted that they can live without expansion. If they do not get it in one way, they must in another, or perish.

As to men's representing women fairly at present, while we hear from men who owe to their wives not only all that is comfortable or graceful, but all that is wise, in the arrangement of their lives, the frequent remark, " You cannot reason with a woman,"— when from those of delicacy, nobleness, and poetic culture, falls the contemptuous phrase " women and children," and that in no light sally of the hour, but in works intended to give a permanent statement of the best experiences,— when not one man, in the million, shall I say? no, not in the hundred million, can rise above the belief that Woman was made *for Man*,— when such traits as these are daily forced upon the attention, can we feel that Man will always do justice to the interests of Woman ? Can we think that he takes a sufficiently discerning and religious view of her office and destiny *ever* to do her justice, except when prompted by sentiment,— accidentally or transiently, that is, for the sentiment will vary according to the relations in which he is placed? The lover, the poet, the artist, are likely to view her nobly. The father and the philosopher have some chance of liberality; the man of the world, the legislator for expediency, none.

Under these circumstances, without attaching importance, in themselves, to the changes demanded by the champions of Woman, we hail them as signs of the times. We would have every arbitrary barrier thrown down. We would have every path laid open to Woman as freely as to Man. Were this done, and a slight temporary fermentation allowed to subside, we should see crystallizations more pure and of more various beauty. We believe the divine energy would pervade nature to a degree unknown in the history of former ages, and that no discordant collision, but a ravishing harmony of the spheres, would ensue.

Yet, then and only then will mankind be ripe for this, when inward and outward freedom for Woman as much as for Man shall be acknowledged as a *right*, not yielded as a concession. As the friend of the negro assumes that one man cannot by right hold another in bondage, so should the friend of Woman assume that Man cannot by right lay even well-meant restrictions on Woman. If the negro be a soul, if the woman be a soul, apparelled in flesh, to one Master only are they accountable. There is but one law for souls, and, if there is to be an interpreter of it, he must come not as man, or son of man, but as son of God.

Were thought and feeling once so far elevated that

Man should esteem himself the brother and friend, but nowise the lord and tutor, of Woman,— were he really bound with her in equal worship,— arrangements as to function and employment would be of no consequence. What Woman needs is not as a woman to act or rule, but as a nature to grow, as an intellect to discern, as a soul to live freely and unimpeded, to unfold such powers as were given her when we left our common home.   If fewer talents were given her, yet if allowed the free and full employment of these, so that she may render back to the giver his own with usury, she will not complain; nay, I dare to say she will bless and rejoice in her earthly birth-place, her earthly lot.   Let us consider what obstructions impede this good era, and what signs give reason to hope that it draws near.

I was talking on this subject with Miranda, a woman, who, if any in the world could, might speak without heat and bitterness of the position of her sex.   Her father was a man who cherished no sentimental reverence for Woman, but a firm belief in the equality of the sexes. She was his eldest child, and came to him at an age when he needed a companion.   From the time she could speak and go alone, he addressed her not as a plaything, but as a living mind.   Among the few verses he ever wrote was a copy addressed to this child, when the first locks were cut from her head; and the reverence expressed on this occasion for that cherished head, he never belied.   It was to him the temple of immortal intellect.   He respected his child, however, too much to be an indulgent parent. He called on her for clear judgment, for courage, for honor and fidelity; in short, for such virtues as he knew. In so far as he possessed the keys to the wonders of this universe, he allowed free use of them to her, and, by the incentive of a high expectation, he forbade, so far as possible, that she should let the privilege lie idle.

Thus this child was early led to feel herself a child of the spirit. She took her place easily, not only in the world of organized being, but in the world of mind. A dignified sense of self-dependence was given as all her portion, and she found it a sure anchor. Herself securely anchored, her relations with others were established with equal security. She was fortunate in a total absence of those charms which might have drawn to her bewildering flatteries, and in a strong electric nature, which repelled those who did not belong to her, and attracted those who did. With men and women her relations were noble,— affectionate without passion, intellectual without coldness. The world was free to her, and she lived freely in it. Outward adversity came, and inward conflict; but that faith and self-respect had early been awakened which must always lead, at last, to an outward serenity and an inward peace.

Of Miranda I had always thought as an example, that the restraints upon the sex were insuperable only to those who think them so, or who noisily strive to break them. She had taken a course of her own, and no man stood in her way. Many of her acts had been unusual, but excited no uproar. Few helped, but none checked her; and the many men who knew her mind and her life, showed to her confidence as to a brother, gentleness as to a sister. And not only refined, but very coarse men approved and aided one in whom they saw resolution and clearness of design. Her mind was often the leading one, always effective.

When I talked with her upon these matters, and had said very much what I have written, she smilingly replied : " And yet we must admit that I have been fortunate, and this should not be. My good father's early trust gave the first bias, and the rest followed, of course. It is true that I have had less outward aid, in after years, than most women; but that is of little consequence. Religion was early awakened in my soul,— a sense that what the soul is capable to ask it must attain, and that, though I might be aided and instructed by others, I must depend on myself as the only constant friend. This self-dependence, which was honored in me, is deprecated as a fault in most women. They are taught to learn their rule from without, not to unfold it from within.

" This is the fault of Man, who is still vain, and wishes to be more important to Woman than, by right, he should be."

" Men have not shown this disposition toward you," I said.

" No; because the position I early was enabled to take was one of self-reliance. And were all women as sure of their wants as I was, the result would be the same. But they are so overloaded with precepts by guardians, who think that nothing is so much to be dreaded for a woman as originality of thought or character, that their minds are impeded by doubts till they lose their chance of fair, free proportions. The difficulty is to get them to the point from which they shall naturally develop self-respect, and learn self-help.

" Once I thought that men would help to forward this state of things more than I do now. I saw so many of them wretched in the connections they had formed in weakness and vanity. They seemed so glad to esteem women whenever they could.

" ' The soft arms of affection,' said one of the most discerning spirits, ' will not suffice for me, unless on them I see the steel bracelets of strength.'

" But early I perceived that men never, in any extreme of despair, wished to be women. On the contrary, they were ever ready to taunt one another, at any sign of weakness, with,

> " ' Art thou not like the women, who,' —

The passage ends various ways, according to the occasion and rhetoric of the speaker. When they admired any woman, they were inclined to speak of her as ' above her sex.' Silently I observed this, and feared it argued a rooted scepticism, which for ages had been fastening on the heart, and which only an age of miracles could eradicate. Ever I have been treated with great sincerity; and I look upon it as a signal instance of this, that. an intimate friend of the other sex said, in a fervent moment, that I ' deserved in some star to be a man.' He was much surprised when I disclosed my view of my position and hopes, when I declared my faith that the feminine side, the side of love, of beauty, of holiness, was now to have its full chance, and that, if either were better, it was better now to be a woman; for even the slightest achievement of good was furthering an especial work of our time. He smiled incredulously. 'She makes the best she can of it,' thought he. 'Let Jews believe the pride of Jewry, but I am of the better sort, and know better.'

"Another used as highest praise, in speaking of a character in literature, the words ' a manly woman.'

"So in the noble passage of Ben Jonson:

> ' I meant the day-star should not brighter ride,
>   Nor shed like influence from its lucent seat;
> I meant she should be courteous, facile, sweet,
>   Free from that solemn vice of greatness, pride;
> I meant each softest virtue there should meet,
>   Fit in that softer bosom to abide,
> Only a learned and a *manly* soul
>   I purposed her, that should with even powers
> The rock, the spindle, and the shears control
>   Of destiny, and spin her own free hours.' "

"Methinks," said I, "you are too fastidious in objecting to this. Jonson, in using the word 'manly,' only meant to heighten the picture of this, the true, the intelligent fate, with one of the deeper colors."

"And yet," said she, "so invariable is the use of this word where a heroic quality is to be described, and I feel so sure that persistence and courage are the most womanly no less than the most manly qualities, that I would exchange these words for others of a larger sense, at the risk of marring the fine tissue of the verse.

Read, ' A heavenward and instructed soul,' and I should
be satisfied.   Let it not be said, wherever there is energy
or creative genius, ' She has a masculine mind.' "

This by no means argues a willing want of generosity
toward Woman.   Man is as generous towards her as he
knows how to be.

Wherever she has herself arisen in national or private
history, and nobly shone forth in any form of excellence,
men have received her, not only willingly, but with triumph.   Their encomiums, indeed, are always, in some
sense, mortifying ; they show too much surprise.   " Can
this be you ? " he cries to the transfigured Cinderella ;
" well, I should never have thought it, but I am very
glad.   We will tell every one that you have ' *surpassed
your sex.*' "

In every-day life, the feelings of the many are stained
with vanity.   Each wishes to be lord in a little world, to
be superior at least over one ; and he does not feel strong
enough to retain a life-long ascendency over a strong
nature.   Only a Theseus could conquer before he wed
the Amazonian queen.   Hercules wished rather to rest
with Dejanira, and received the poisoned robe as a fit
guerdon.   The tale should be interpreted to all those
who seek repose with the weak.

But not only is Man vain and fond of power, but the
same want of development, which thus affects him mor-
ally, prevents his intellectually discerning the destiny of
Woman.   The boy wants no woman, but only a girl to
play ball with him, and mark his pocket handkerchief.

Thus, in Schiller's Dignity of Woman, beautiful as the poem is, there is no "grave and perfect man," but only a great boy to be softened and restrained by the influence of girls. Poets — the elder brothers of their race — have usually seen further; but what can you expect of every-day men, if Schiller was not more prophetic as to what women must be? Even with Richter, one foremost thought about a wife was that she would "cook him something good." But as this is a delicate subject, and we are in constant danger of being accused of slighting what are called "the functions," let me say, in behalf of Miranda and myself, that we have high respect for those who "cook something good," who create and preserve fair order in houses, and prepare therein the shining raiment for worthy inmates, worthy guests. Only these "functions" must not be a drudgery, or enforced necessity, but a part of life. Let Ulysses drive the beeves home, while Penelope there piles up the fragrant loaves; they are both well employed if these be done in thought and love, willingly. But Penelope is no more meant for a baker or weaver solely, than Ulysses for a cattle-herd.

The sexes should not only correspond to and appreciate, but prophesy to one another. In individual instances this happens. Two persons love in one another the future good which they aid one another to unfold. This is imperfectly or rarely done in the general life. Man has gone but little way; now he is waiting to see whether Woman can keep step with him; but, instead of calling out, like a good brother, "You can do

it, if you only think so," or impersonally, " Any one
can do what he tries to do ; " he often discourages with
school-boy brag : " Girls can't do that; girls can't play
ball." But let any one defy their taunts, break through
and be brave and secure, they rend the air with shouts.

This fluctuation was obvious in a narrative I have
lately seen, the story of the life of Countess Emily
Plater, the heroine of the last revolution in Poland.
The dignity, the purity, the concentrated resolve, the
calm, deep enthusiasm, which yet could, when occasion
called, sparkle up a holy, an indignant fire, make of this
young maiden the figure I want for my frontispiece.
Her portrait is to be seen in the book, a gentle shadow
of her soul. Short was the career. Like the Maid of
Orleans, she only did enough to verify her credentials,
and then passed from a scene on which she was, probably, a premature apparition.

When the young girl joined the army, where the report
of her exploits had preceded her, she was received in a
manner that marks the usual state of feeling. Some of
the officers were disappointed at her quiet manners ; that
she had not the air and tone of a stage-heroine. They
thought she could not have acted heroically unless in
buskins ; had no idea that such deeds only showed the
habit of her mind. Others talked of the delicacy of her
sex, advised her to withdraw from perils and dangers,
and had no comprehension of the feelings within her
breast that made this impossible. The gentle irony of
her reply to these self-constituted tutors (not one of
whom showed himself her equal in conduct or reason), is

as good as her indignant reproof at a later period to the general, whose perfidy ruined all.

But though, to the mass of these men, she was an embarrassment and a puzzle, the nobler sort viewed her with a tender enthusiasm worthy of her. "Her name," said her biographer, "is known throughout Europe. I paint her character that she may be as widely loved."

With pride, he shows her freedom from all personal affections ; that, though tender and gentle in an uncommon degree, there was no room for a private love in her consecrated life. She inspired those who knew her with a simple energy of feeling like her own. "We have seen," they felt, "a woman worthy the name, capable of all sweet affections, capable of stern virtue."

It is a fact worthy of remark, that all these revolutions in favor of liberty have produced female champions that share the same traits, but Emily alone has found a biographer. Only a near friend could have performed for her this task, for the flower was reared in feminine seclusion, and the few and simple traits of her history before her appearance in the field could only have been known to the domestic circle. Her biographer has gathered them up with a brotherly devotion.

No ! Man is not willingly ungenerous. He wants faith and love, because he is not yet himself an elevated being. He cries, with sneering scepticism, "Give us a sign." But if the sign appears, his eyes glisten, and he offers not merely approval, but homage.

The severe nation which taught that the happiness of the race was forfeited through the fault of a Woman, and

showed its thought of what sort of regard Man owed her,
by making him accuse her on the first question to his
God, — who gave her to the patriarch as a handmaid,
and, by the Mosaical law, bound her to allegiance like a
serf, — even they greeted, with solemn rapture, all
great and holy women as heroines, prophetesses, judges
in Israel; and, if they made Eve listen to the serpent,
gave Mary as a bride to the Holy Spirit. In other
nations it has been the same down to our day. To
the Woman who could conquer a triumph was awarded.
And not only those whose strength was recommended to
the heart by association with goodness and beauty, but
those who were bad, if they were steadfast and strong,
had their claims allowed. In any age a Semiramis, an
Elizabeth of England, a Catharine of Russia, makes her
place good, whether in a large or small circle. How
has a little wit, a little genius, been celebrated in a
Woman! What an intellectual triumph was that of the
lonely Aspasia, and how heartily acknowledged! She,
indeed, met a Pericles. But what annalist, the rudest
of men, the most plebeian of husbands, will spare from
his page one of the few anecdotes of Roman women —
Sappho! Eloisa! The names are of threadbare celeb-
rity. Indeed, they were not more suitably met in their
own time than the Countess Colonel Plater on her first
joining the army. They had much to mourn, and their
great impulses did not find due scope. But with time
enough, space enough, their kindred appear on the
scene. Across the ages, forms lean, trying to touch the
hem of their retreating robes. The youth here by my

side cannot be weary of the fragments from the life of
Sappho. He will not. believe they are not addressed to
himself, or that he to whom they were addressed could
be ungrateful. A recluse of high powers devotes himself to understand and explain the thought of Eloisa;
he asserts her vast superiority in soul and genius to her
master ; he curses the fate that casts his lot in another
age than hers. He could have understood her; he would
have been to her a friend, such as Abelard never could.
And this one Woman he could have loved and reverenced,
and she, alas ! lay cold in her grave hundreds of years
ago. His sorrow is truly pathetic. These responses,
that come too late to give joy, are as tragic as anything
we know, and yet the tears of later ages glitter as they
fall on Tasso's prison bars. And we know how elevating
to the captive is the security that somewhere an intelligence must answer to his.

The Man habitually most narrow towards Woman will
be flushed, as by the worst assault on Christianity, if you
say it has made no improvement in her condition. Indeed, those most opposed to new acts in her favor, are
jealous of the reputation of those which have been
done.

We will not speak of the enthusiasm excited by actresses, improvisatrici, female singers, — for here mingles
the charm of beauty and grace, — but female authors, even
learned women, if not insufferably ugly and slovenly,
from the Italian professor's daughter who taught behind
the curtain, down to Mrs. Carter and Madame Dacier,
are sure of an admiring audience, and, what is far bet-

ter, chance to use what they have learned, and to learn more, if they can once get a platform on which to stand.

But how to get this platform, or how to make it of reasonably easy access, is the difficulty. Plants of great vigor will almost always struggle into blossom, despite impediments. But there should be encouragement, and a free genial atmosphere for those of more timid sort, fair play for each in its own kind. Some are like the little, delicate flowers which love to hide in the dripping mosses, by the sides of mountain torrents, or in the shade of tall trees. But others require an open field, a rich and loosened soil, or they never show their proper hues.

It may be said that Man does not have his fair play either; his energies are repressed and distorted by the interposition of artificial obstacles. Ay, but he himself has put them there; they have grown out of his own imperfections. If there *is* a misfortune in Woman's lot, it is in obstacles being interposed by men, which do *not* mark her state ; and, if they express her past ignorance, do not her present needs. As every Man is of Woman born, she has slow but sure means of redress ; yet the sooner a general justness of thought makes smooth the path, the better.

Man is of Woman born, and her face bends over him in infancy with an expression he can never quite forget. Eminent men have delighted to pay tribute to this image, and it is an hackneyed observation, that most men of genius boast some remarkable development in the mother. The rudest tar brushes off a tear with his coat-sleeve at the hallowed name.   The other day, I met a decrepit old man of seventy, on a journey, who challenged the stage company to guess where he was going.   They guessed aright, " To see your mother."   " Yes," said he," she is ninety-two, but has good eyesight still, they say.   I have not seen her these forty years, and I thought I could not die in peace without."   I should have liked his picture painted as a companion-piece to that of a boisterous little boy, whom I saw attempt to declaim at a school exhibition —

> " O that those lips had language !   Life has passed
> With me but roughly since I heard thee last."

He got but very little way before sudden tears shamed him from the stage.

Some gleams of the same expression which shone down upon his infancy, angelically pure and benign, visit Man again with hopes of pure love, of a holy marriage. Or, if not before, in the eyes of the mother of his child they again are seen, and dim fancies pass before his mind, that Woman may not have been born for him alone, but have come from heaven, a commissioned soul, a messenger of truth and love ; that she can only make for him a home in which he may lawfully repose, in so far as she is

> " True to the kindred points of Heaven and home."

In gleams, in dim fancies, this thought visits the mind of common men.   It is soon obscured by the mists of sensuality, the dust of routine, and he thinks it was only some meteor or ignis fatuus that shone.   But, as a

Rosicrucian lamp, it burns unwearied, though condemned
to the solitude of tombs; and to its permanent life, as to
every truth, each age has in some form borne witness.
For the truths, which visit the minds of careless men
only in fitful gleams, shine with radiant clearness into
those of the poet, the priest, and the artist.

Whatever may have been the domestic manners of the
ancients, the idea of Woman was nobly manifested in
their mythologies and poems, where she appears as Sita
in the Ramayana, a form of tender purity; as the Egyp-
tian Isis,* of divine wisdom never yet surpassed. In
Egypt, too, the Sphynx, walking the earth with lion
tread, looked out upon its marvels in the calm, inscrut-
able beauty of a virgin's face, and the Greek could only
add wings to the great emblem. In Greece, Ceres and
Proserpine, significantly termed " the great goddesses,"
were seen seated side by side. They needed not to rise
for any worshipper or any change; they were prepared
for all things, as those initiated to their mysteries knew.
More obvious is the meaning of these three forms, the
Diana, Minerva, and Vesta. Unlike in the expression
of their beauty, but alike in this,— that each was self-
sufficing. Other forms were only accessories and illustrations, none the complement to one like these. Another
might, indeed, be the companion, and the Apollo and
Diana set off one another's beauty. Of the Vesta, it is
to be observed, that not only deep-eyed, deep-discerning
Greece, but ruder Rome, who represents the only form
of good man (the always busy warrior) that could be

* For an adequate description of the Isis, see Appendix A.

indifferent to Woman, confided the permanence of its glory
to a tutelary goddess, and her wisest legislator spoke of
meditation as a nymph.

Perhaps in Rome the neglect of Woman was a reaction
on the manners of Etruria, where the priestess Queen,
warrior Queen, would seem to have been so usual a character.

An instance of the noble Roman marriage, where the
stern and calm nobleness of the nation was common to
both; we see in the historic page through the little that
is told us of Brutus and Portia.   Shakspeare has
seized on the relation in its native lineaments, harmoniz-
ing the particular with the universal; and, while it is
conjugal love, and no other, making it unlike the same
relation as seen in Cymbeline, or Othello, even as one
star differeth from another in glory.

> " By that great vow
> Which did incorporate and make us one,
> Unfold to me, yourself, your other half,
> Why you are heavy.   *   *   *
> Dwell I but in the suburbs
> Of your good pleasure ?   If it be no more,
> Portia is Brutus' harlot, not his wife."

Mark the sad majesty of his tone in answer.   Who
would not have lent a life-long credence to that voice of
honor ?

> " You are my true and honorable wife ;
> As dear to me as are the ruddy drops
> That visit this sad heart."

It is the same voice that tells the moral of his life in
the last words —

" Countrymen,
My heart doth joy, that, yet in all my life,
I found no man but he was true to me."

It was not wonderful that it should be so.

Shakspeare, however, was not content to let Portia
rest her plea for confidence on the essential nature of the
marriage bond:

" I grant I am a woman ; but withal,
A woman that lord Brutus took to wife.
I grant I am a woman ; but withal,
A woman well reputed — Cato's daughter.
Think you I am *no stronger than my sex*,
Being so fathered and so husbanded ? "

And afterward in the very scene where Brutus is suffering under that " insupportable and touching loss," the
death of his wife, Cassius pleads —

" Have you not love enough to bear with me,
When that rash humor which my mother gave me
Makes me forgetful ?
Brutus. — Yes, Cassius, and henceforth,
When you are over-earnest with your Brutus,
He'll think your mother chides, and leaves you so."

As indeed it was a frequent belief among the ancients,
as with our Indians, that the *body* was inherited from
the mother, the *soul* from the father. As in that noble
passage of Ovid, already quoted, where Jupiter, as his
divine synod are looking down on the funeral pyre of
Hercules, thus triumphs —

" Nec nisi *maternâ* Vulcanum parte potentem,
Sentiet. Aeternum est, à me quod traxit, et expers

Atque immune necis, nullaque domabile flamma
Idque ego defunctum terrâ cœlestibus oris
Accipiam, cunctisque meum lætabile factum
Dis fore confido.

" The part alone of gross *maternal* frame
    Fire shall devour ; while that from me he drew
    Shall live immortal and its force renew ;
    That, when he 's dead, I 'll raise to realms above ;
    Let all the powers the righteous act approve."

It is indeed a god speaking of his union with an
earthly Woman, but it expresses the common Roman
thought as to marriage,— the same which permitted a
man to lend his wife to a friend, as if she were a chattel.

" She dwelt but in the suburbs of his good pleasure."

Yet the same city, as I have said, leaned on the worship
of Vesta, the Preserver, and in later times was devoted
to that of Isis.   In Sparta, thought, in this respect as in
all others, was expressed in the characters of real life,
and the women of Sparta were as much Spartans as the
men.   The " citoyen, citoyenne " of France was here
actualized.   Was not the calm equality they enjoyed as
honorable as the devotion of chivalry ?   They intel-
ligently shared the ideal life of their nation.

Like the men they felt

" Honor gone, all 's gone :
Better never have been born."

They were the true friends of men.   The Spartan,
surely, would not think that he received only his body
from his mother.   The sage, had he lived in that community, could not have thought the souls of " vain and

foppish men will be degraded after death to the forms of women; and, if they do not then make great efforts to retrieve themselves, will become birds."

(By the way, it is very expressive of the hard intellectuality of the merely *mannish* mind, to speak thus of birds, chosen always by the *feminine* poet as the symbols of his fairest thoughts.)

We are told of the Greek nations in general, that Woman occupied there an infinitely lower place than Man. It is difficult to believe this, when we see such range and dignity of thought on the subject in the mythologies, and find the poets producing such ideals as Cassandra, Iphigenia, Antigone, Macaria; where Sibylline priestesses told the oracle of the highest god, and he could not be content to reign with a court of fewer than nine muses. Even Victory wore a female form.

But, whatever were the facts of daily life, I cannot complain of the age and nation which represents its thought by such a symbol as I see before me at this moment. It is a zodiac of the busts of gods and goddesses, arranged in pairs. The circle breathes the music of a heavenly order. Male and female heads are distinct in expression, but equal in beauty, strength and calmness. Each male head is that of a brother and a king, — each female of a sister and a queen. Could the thought thus expressed be lived out, there would be nothing more to be desired. There would be unison in variety, congeniality in difference.

Coming nearer our own time, we find religion and poetry no less true in their revelations. The rude man,

just disengaged from the sod, the Adam, accuses Woman
to his God, and records her disgrace to their posterity.
He is not ashamed to write that he could be drawn from
heaven by one beneath him,— one made, he says, from
but a small part of himself. But in the same nation,
educated by time, instructed by a succession of prophets,
we find Woman in as high a position as she has ever occupied. No figure that has ever arisen to greet our eyes
has been received with more fervent reverence than that
of the Madonna. Heine calls her the *Dame du Comp-
toir* of the Catholic church, and this jeer well expresses
a serious truth.

And not only this holy and significant image was worshipped by the pilgrim, and the favorite subject of the
artist, but it exercised an immediate influence on the
destiny of the sex. The empresses who embraced the
cross converted sons and husbands. Whole calendars
of female saints, heroic dames of chivalry, binding the
emblem of faith on the heart of the best-beloved, and
wasting the bloom of youth in separation and loneliness,
for the sake of duties they thought it religion to assume,
with innumerable forms of poesy, trace their lineage to
this one. Nor, however imperfect may be the action,
in our day, of the faith thus expressed, and though we
can scarcely think it nearer this ideal than that of India
or Greece was near their ideal, is it in vain that the truth
has been recognized, that Woman is not only a part of
Man, bone of his bone, and flesh of his flesh, born that
men might not be lonely — but that women are in themselves possessors of and possessed by immortal souls.

This truth undoubtedly received a greater outward stability from the belief of the church that the earthly parent of the Saviour of souls was a woman.

The Assumption of the Virgin, as painted by sublime artists, as also Petrarch's Hymn to the Madonna,* cannot have spoken to the world wholly without result, yet oftentimes those who had ears heard not.

See upon the nations the influence of this powerful example. In Spain look only at the ballads. Woman in these is "very Woman;" she is the betrothed, the bride, the spouse of Man; there is on her no hue of the philosopher, the heroine, the savante, but she looks great and noble. Why? Because she is also, through her deep devotion, the betrothed of Heaven. Her upturned eyes have drawn down the light that casts a radiance round her. See only such a ballad as that of "Lady Teresa's Bridal," where the Infanta, given to the Moorish bridegroom, calls down the vengeance of Heaven on his unhallowed passion, and thinks it not too much to expiate by a life in the cloister the involuntary stain upon her princely youth.† It was this constant sense of claims above those of earthly love or happiness that made the Spanish lady who shared this spirit a guerdon to be won by toils and blood and constant purity, rather than a chattel to be bought for pleasure and service.

Germany did not need to *learn* a high view of Woman; it was inborn in that race. Woman was to the Teuton warrior his priestess, his friend, his sister,— in truth, a wife. And the Christian statues of noble pairs, as they

* Appendix B.   † Appendix C.

lie above their graves in stone, expressing the meaning
of all the by-gone pilgrimage by hands folded in mutual
prayer, yield not a nobler sense of the place and powers
of Woman than belonged to the *altvater* day.   The holy
love of Christ which summoned them, also, to choose
" the better part — that which could not be taken from
them," refined and hallowed in this nation a native faith ;
thus showing that it was not the warlike spirit alone that
left the Latins so barbarous in this respect.

But the Germans, taking so kindly to this thought,
did it the more justice.   The idea of Woman in their
literature is expressed both to a greater height and depth
than elsewhere.

I will give as instances the themes of three ballads :

One is upon a knight who had always the name of the
Virgin on his lips.   This protected him all his life
through, in various and beautiful modes, both from sin
and other dangers; and, when he died, a plant sprang
from his grave, which so gently whispered the Ave
Maria that none could pass it by with an unpurified heart.

Another is one of the legends of the famous Dra-
chenfels.   A maiden, one of the earliest converts to
Christianity, was carried by the enraged populace to this
dread haunt of " the dragon's fabled brood," to be
their prey.   She was left alone, but undismayed, for she
knew in whom she trusted.   So, when the dragons
came rushing towards her, she showed them a crucifix
and they crouched reverently at her feet.   Next day the
people came, and, seeing these wonders, were all turned to
the faith which exalts the lowly.

The third I have in mind is another of the Rhine legends. A youth is sitting with the maid he loves on the shore of an isle, her fairy kingdom, then perfumed by the blossoming grape-vines which draped its bowers. They are happy; all blossoms with them, and life promises its richest wine. A boat approaches on the tide; it pauses at their feet. It brings, perhaps, some joyous message, fresh dew for their flowers, fresh light on the wave. No! it is the usual check on such great happiness. The father of the count departs for the crusade; will his son join him, or remain to rule their domain, and wed her he loves? Neither of the affianced pair hesitates a moment. "I must go with my father," — "Thou must go with thy father." It was one thought, one word. "I will be here again," he said, "when these blossoms have turned to purple grapes." "I hope so," she sighed, while the prophetic sense said "no."

And there she waited, and the grapes ripened, and were gathered into the vintage, and he came not. Year after year passed thus, and no tidings; yet still she waited.

He, meanwhile, was in a Moslem prison. Long he languished there without hope, till, at last, his patron saint appeared in vision and announced his release, but only on condition of his joining the monastic order for the service of the saint.

And so his release was effected, and a safe voyage home given. And once more he sets sail upon the Rhine. The maiden, still watching beneath the vines, sees at last the object of all this patient love approach —

approach, but not to touch the strand to which she, with
outstretched arms, has rushed.   He dares not trust himself to land, but in low, heart-broken tones, tells her of
Heaven's will ; and that he, in obedience to his vow, is
now on his way to a convent on the river-bank, there to
pass the rest of his earthly life in the service of the
shrine.   And then he turns his boat, and floats away from
her and hope of any happiness in this world, but urged,
as he believes, by the breath of Heaven.

The maiden stands appalled, but she dares not murmur, and cannot hesitate long.   She also bids them prepare her boat.   She follows her lost love to the convent
gate, requests an interview with the abbot, and devotes
her Elysian isle, where vines had ripened their ruby
fruit in vain for her, to the service of the monastery
where her love was to serve.   Then, passing over to the
nunnery opposite, she takes the veil, and meets her
betrothed at the altar ; and for a life-long union, if not
the one they had hoped in earlier years.

Is not this sorrowful story of a lofty beauty?   Does
it not show a sufficiently high view of Woman, of Marriage?   This is commonly the chivalric, still more the
German view.

Yet, wherever there was a balance in the mind of Man,
of sentiment with intellect, such a result was sure.   The
Greek Xenophon has not only painted us a sweet picture
of the domestic Woman, in his Economics, but in the
Cyropedia has given, in the picture of Panthea, a view
of Woman which no German picture can surpass, whether
lonely and quiet with veiled lids, the temple of a vestal

loveliness, or with eyes flashing, and hair flowing to the
free wind, cheering on the hero to fight for his God, his
country, or whatever name his duty might bear at the
time. This picture I shall copy by and by. Yet Xenophon grew up in the same age with him who makes
Iphigenia say to Achilles,

" Better a thousand women should perish than one man cease to
see the light."

This was the vulgar Greek sentiment. Xenophon, aim-
ing at the ideal Man, caught glimpses of the ideal
Woman also. From the figure of a Cyrus the Pantheas
stand not afar. They do not in thought; they would
not in life.

I could swell the catalogue of instances far beyond the
reader's patience. But enough have been brought forward to show that, though there has been great disparity
betwixt the nations as between individuals in their culture on this point, yet the idea of Woman has always cast
some rays and often been forcibly represented.

Far less has Woman to complain that she has not had
her share of power. This, in all ranks of society, except
the lowest, has been hers to the extent that vanity
would crave, far beyond what wisdom would accept. In
the very lowest, where Man, pressed by poverty, sees in
Woman only the partner of toils and cares, and cannot
hope, scarcely has an idea of, a comfortable home, he
often maltreats her, and is less influenced by her.
In all ranks, those who are gentle and uncomplaining,
too candid to intrigue, too delicate to encroach, suffer

much. They suffer long, and are kind; verily, they
have their reward. But wherever Man is sufficiently
raised above extreme poverty, or brutal stupidity,
to care for the comforts of the fireside, or the bloom
and ornament of life, Woman has always power enough,
if she choose to exert it, and is usually disposed to do
so, in proportion to her ignorance and childish vanity. Unacquainted with the importance of life and its
purposes, trained to a selfish coquetry and love of
petty power, she does not look beyond the pleasure of
making herself felt at the moment, and governments are
shaken and commerce broken up to gratify the pique of
a female favorite. The English shopkeeper's wife does
not vote, but it is for her interest that the politician can-
vasses by the coarsest flattery. France suffers no woman
on her throne, but her proud nobles kiss the dust at the
feet of Pompadour and Dubarry; for such flare in the
lighted foreground where a Roland would modestly aid in
the closet. Spain (that same Spain which sang of Ximena
and the Lady Teresa) shuts up her women in the care of
duennas, and allows them no book but the breviary; but
the ruin follows only the more surely from the worthless
favorite of a worthless queen. Relying on mean precau-
tions, men indeed cry peace, peace, where there is no peace.

It is not the transient breath of poetic incense that
women want; each can receive that from a lover. It is
not life-long sway; it needs but to become a coquette, a
shrew, or a good cook, to be sure of that. It is not
money, nor notoriety, nor the badges of authority which
men have appropriated to themselves. If demands, made

in their behalf, lay stress on any of these particulars, those who make them have not searched deeply into the need.   The want is for that which at once includes these and precludes them ; which would not be forbidden power, lest there be temptation to steal and misuse it ; which would not have the mind perverted by flattery from a worthiness of esteem ; it is for that which is the birthright of every being capable of receiving it, — the freedom, the religious, the intelligent freedom of the universe to use its means, to learn its secret, as far as Nature has enabled them, with God alone for their guide and their judge.

Ye cannot believe it, men ; but the only reason why women ever assume what is more appropriate to you, is because you prevent them from finding out what is fit for themselves.   Were they free, were they wise fully to develop the strength and beauty of Woman ; they would never wish to be men, or man-like.   The well-instructed moon flies not from her orbit to seize on the glories of her partner.   No ; for she knows that one law rules, one heaven contains, one universe replies to them alike.   It is with women as with the slave :

> " Vor dem Sklaven, wenn er die Kette bricht,
> Vor dem freien Menschen erzittert nicht."

Tremble not before the free man, but before the slave who has chains to break.

In slavery, acknowledged slavery, women are on a par with men.   Each is a work-tool, an article of property, no more !   In perfect freedom, such as is painted in Olympus, in Swedenborg's angelic state, in the heaven where there is no marrying nor giving in marriage, each is a purified intelligence, an enfranchised soul,— no less.

> " Jene himmlische Gestalten
> Sie fragen nicht nach Mann und Weib,
> Und keine kleider, keine Falten
> Umgeben den verklarten Leib."

The child who sang this was a prophetic form, expressive of the longing for a state of perfect freedom, pure love. She could not remain here, but was translated to another air. And it may be that the air of this earth will never be so tempered that such can bear it long. But, while they stay, they must bear testimony to the truth they are constituted to demand.

That an era approaches which shall approximate nearer to such a temper than any has yet done, there are many tokens; indeed, so many that only a few of the most prominent can here be enumerated.

The reigns of Elizabeth of England and Isabella of Castile foreboded this era. They expressed the beginning of the new state, while they forwarded its progress. These were strong characters, and in harmony with the wants of their time. One showed that this strength did not unfit a woman for the duties of a wife and a mother; the other, that it could enable her to live and die alone, a wide energetic life, a courageous death. Elizabeth is certainly no pleasing example. In rising above the weakness, she did not lay aside the foibles ascribed to her sex; but her strength must be respected now, as it was in her own time.

Mary Stuart and Elizabeth seem types, moulded by

the spirit of the time, and placed upon an elevated platform, to show to the coming ages Woman such as the conduct and wishes of Man in general is likely to make her.   The first shows Woman lovely even to allurement; quick in apprehension and weak in judgment; with grace and dignity of sentiment, but no principle; credulous and indiscreet, yet artful; capable of sudden greatness or of crime, but not of a steadfast wisdom, nor self-restraining virtue.   The second reveals Woman half-emancipated and jealous of her freedom, such as she has figured before or since in many a combative attitude, mannish, not equally manly; strong and prudent more than great or wise; able to control vanity, and the wish to rule through coquetry and passion, but not to resign these dear deceits from the very foundation, as unworthy a being capable of truth and nobleness.   Elizabeth, taught by adversity, put on her virtues as armor, more than produced them in a natural order from her soul.   The time and her position called on her to act the wise sovereign, and she was proud that she could do so, but her tastes and inclinations would have led her to act the weak woman.   She was without magnanimity of any kind.

We may accept as an omen for ourselves that it was Isabella who furnished Columbus with the means of coming hither.   This land must pay back its debt to Woman, without whose aid it would not have been brought into alliance with the civilized world.

A graceful and meaning figure is that introduced to us by Mr. Prescott, in the Conquest of Mexico, in the

Indian girl Marina, who accompanied Cortez, and was
his interpreter in all the various difficulties of his career.
She stood at his side, on the walls of the besieged palace,
to plead with her enraged countrymen. By her name
he was known in New Spain, and, after the conquest, her
gentle intercession was often of avail to the conquered.
The poem of the Future may be read in some features of
the story of " Malinche."

The influence of Elizabeth on literature was real,
though, by sympathy with its finer productions, she was
no more entitled to give name to an era than Queen
Anne.   It was simply that the fact of having a female
sovereign on the throne affected the course of a writer's
thoughts.   In this sense, the presence of a woman on the
throne always makes its mark.   Life is lived before the
eyes of men, by which their imaginations are stimulated
as to the possibilities of Woman.   " We will die for our
king, Maria Theresa," cry the wild warriors, clashing
their swords ; and the sounds vibrate through the poems
of that generation.   The range of female character in
Spenser alone might content us for one period.   Britomart and Belphœbe have as much room on the canvas as
Florimel ; and, where this is the case, the haughtiest
Amazon will not murmur that Una should be felt to be
the fairest type.

Unlike as was the English queen to a fairy queen, we
may yet conceive that it was the image of *a* queen before
the poet's mind that called up this splendid court of
women.   Shakspeare's range is also great ; but he has
left out the heroic characters, such as the Macaria of

Greece, the Britomart of Spenser. Ford and Massinger
have, in this respect, soared to a higher flight of feeling
than he. It was the holy and heroic Woman they
most loved, and if they could not paint an Imogen, a
Desdemona, a Rosalind, yet, in those of a stronger mould,
they showed a higher ideal, though with so much less
poetic power to embody it, than we see in Portia or Isabella. The simple truth of Cordelia, indeed, is of this
sort. The beauty of Cordelia is neither male nor female;
it is the beauty of virtue.

The ideal of love and marriage rose high in the mind
of all the Christian nations who were capable of grave
and deep feeling. We may take as examples of its English aspect the lines,

> " I could not love thee, dear, so much,
> Loved I not honor more."

Or the address of the Commonwealth's man to his wife,
as she looked out from the Tower window to see him, for
the last time, on his way to the scaffold. He stood up in
the cart, waved his hat, and cried, " To Heaven, my
love, to Heaven, and leave you in the storm ! "

Such was the love of faith and honor, — a love which
stopped, like Colonel Hutchinson's, " on this side idolatry," because it was religious. The meeting of two
such souls Donne describes as giving birth to an " abler
soul."

Lord Herbert wrote to his love,

> " Were not our souls immortal made,
> Our equal loves can make them such."

In the "Broken Heart," of Ford, Penthea, a character which engages my admiration even more deeply than the famous one of Calanthe, is made to present to the mind the most beautiful picture of what these relations should be in their purity. Her life cannot sustain the violation of what she so clearly feels.

Shakspeare, too, saw that, in true love, as in fire, the utmost ardor is coïncident with the utmost purity. It is a true lover that exclaims in the agony of Othello,

"If thou art false, O then Heaven mocks itself!"

The son, framed, like Hamlet, to appreciate truth in all the beauty of relations, sinks into deep melancholy when he finds his natural expectations disappointed. He has no other. She to whom he gave the name, disgraces from his heart's shrine all the sex.

"Frailty, thy name is Woman."

It is because a Hamlet could find cause to say so, that I have put the line, whose stigma has never been removed, at the head of my work. But, as a lover, surely Hamlet would not have so far mistaken, as to have finished with such a conviction. He would have felt the faith of Othello, and that faith could not, in his more dispassionate mind, have been disturbed by calumny.

In Spain, this thought is arrayed in a sublimity which belongs to the sombre and passionate genius of the nation. Calderon's Justina resists all the temptation of the Demon, and raises her lover, with her, above the sweet lures of mere temporal happiness. Their marriage is vowed at the stake; their souls are liberated together by the martyr flame into "a purer state of sensation and existence."

In Italy, the great poets wove into their lives an ideal love which answered to the highest wants. It included those of the intellect and the affections, for it was a love of spirit for spirit. It was not ascetic, or superhuman, but, interpreting all things, gave their proper beauty to details of the common life, the common day. The poet spoke of his love, not as a flower to place in his bosom, or hold carelessly in his hand, but as a light toward which he must find wings to fly, or " a stair to heaven." He delighted to speak of her, not only as the bride of his heart, but the mother of his soul; for he saw that, in cases where the right direction had been taken, the greater delicacy of her frame and stillness of her life left her more open than is Man to spiritual influx. So he did not look upon her as betwixt him and earth, to serve his temporal needs, but, rather, betwixt him and heaven, to purify his affections and lead him to wisdom through love. He sought, in her, not so much the Eve as the Madonna.

In these minds the thought, which gleams through all the legends of chivalry, shines in broad intellectual effulgence, not to be misinterpreted; and their thought is reverenced by the world, though it lies far from the practice of the world as yet, — so far that it seems as though a gulf of death yawned between.

Even with such men the practice was, often, widely different from the mental faith. I say mental; for if the heart were thoroughly alive with it, the practice could not be dissonant.   Lord Herbert's was a marriage of convention, made for him at fifteen; he was not discontented with it, but looked only to the advantages it brought of perpetuating his family on the basis of a great fortune. He paid, in act, what he considered a dutiful attention to the bond; his thoughts travelled elsewhere; and while forming a high ideal of the companionship of minds in marriage, he seems never to have doubted that its realization must be postponed to some other state of being. Dante, almost immediately after the death of Beatrice, married a lady chosen for him by his friends, and Boccaccio, in describing the miseries that attended, in this case,

"The form of an union where union is none,"

speaks as if these were inevitable to the connection, and as if the scholar and poet, especially, could expect nothing but misery and obstruction in a domestic partnership with Woman.

Centuries have passed since, but civilized Europe is still in a transition state about marriage; not only in practice but in thought.   It is idle to speak with contempt of the nations where polygamy is an institution, or seraglios a custom, while practices far more debasing haunt, well-nigh fill, every city and every town, and so far as union of one with one is believed to be the only pure form of marriage, a great majority of societies and individuals are still doubtful whether the earthly bond must be a meeting of souls, or only supposes a contract of convenience and utility.   Were Woman established in the rights of an immortal being, this could not be. She would not, in some countries, be given away by her father, with scarcely more respect for her feelings than is shown by the Indian chief, who sells his daughter for a horse, and beats her if she runs away from her new home. Nor, in societies where her choice is left free, would she be perverted, by the current of opinion that seizes her, into the belief that she must marry, if it be only to find a protector, and a home of her own. Neither would Man, if he thought the connection of permanent importance, form it so lightly. He would not deem it a trifle, that he was to enter into the closest relations with another soul, which, if not eternal in themselves, must eternally affect his growth. Neither, did he believe Woman capable of friendship,* would he, by rash haste, lose the chance of finding a friend in the person who might, probably, live half a century by his side. Did love, to his mind, stretch forth into infinity, he would not miss his chance of its revelations, that he might the sooner rest from his weariness by a bright fireside, and secure a sweet and graceful attendant " devoted to him alone." Were he a step higher, he would not carelessly enter into a relation where he might not be able to do the duty of a friend, as well as a protector from external ill, to the other party, and have a being in his power pining for sympathy, intelligence and aid, that he could not give.

What deep communion, what real intercourse is im-

---

* See Appendix D, Spinoza's view.

plied in sharing the joys and cares of parentage, when any degree of equality is admitted between the parties ! It is true that, in a majority of instances, the man looks upon his wife as an adopted child, and places her to the other children in the relation of nurse or governess, rather than that of parent. Her influence with them is sure ; but she misses the education which should enlighten that influence, by being thus treated. It is the order of nature that children should complete the education, moral and mental, of parents, by making them think what is needed for the best culture of human beings, and conquer all faults and impulses that interfere with their giving this to these dear objects, who represent the world to them. Father and mother should assist one another to learn what is required for this sublime priesthood of Nature. But, for this, a religious recognition of equality is required.

Where this thought of equality begins to diffuse itself, it is shown in four ways.

First ; — The household partnership. In our country, the woman looks for a " smart but kind " husband ; the man for a " capable, sweet-tempered " wife. The man furnishes the house ; the woman regulates it. Their relation is one of mutual esteem, mutual dependence. Their talk is of business ; their affection shows itself by practical kindness. They know that life goes more smoothly and cheerfully to each for the other's aid ; they are grateful and content. The wife praises her husband as a " good provider ; " the husband, in return, com-

pliments her as a " capital housekeeper." This relation
is good so far as it goes.

Next comes a closer tie, which takes the form either of
mutual idolatry or of intellectual companionship. The
first, we suppose, is to no one a pleasing subject of con-
templaticn. The parties weaken and narrow one another;
they lock the gate against all the glories of the universe,
that they may live in a cell together. To themselves
they seem the only wise ; to all others, steeped in infatu-
ation ; the gods smile as they look forward to the crisis
of cure ; to men, the woman seems an unlovely syren ; to
women, the man an effeminate boy.

The other form, of intellectual companionship, has
become more and more frequent. Men engaged in public life, literary men, and artists, have often found in
their wives companions and confidants in thought no less
than in feeling. And, as the intellectual development of
Woman has spread wider and risen higher, they have,
not unfrequently, shared the same employment; as in
the case of Roland and his wife, who were friends in the
household and in the nation's councils, read, regulated
home affairs, or prepared public documents together,
indifferently. It is very pleasant, in letters begun by
Roland and finished by his wife, to see the harmony of
mind, and the difference of nature ; one thought, but
various ways of treating it.

This is one of the best instances of a marriage of
friendship. It was only friendship, whose basis was
esteem ; probably neither party knew love, except by
name. Roland was a good man, worthy to esteem, and be

esteemed ; his wife as deserving of admiration as able to do without it.

Madame Roland is the fairest specimen we yet have of her class ; as clear to discern her aim, as valiant to pursue it, as Spenser's Britomart ; austerely set apart from all that did not belong to her, whether as Woman or as mind. She is an antetype of a class to which the coming time will afford a field — the Spartan matron, brought by the culture of the age of books to intellectual consciousness and expansion. Self-sufficingness, strength, and clear-sightedness were, in her, combined with a power of deep and calm affection. She, too, would have given a son or husband the device for his shield, " Return with it or upon it ; " and this, not because she loved little, but much. The page of her life is one of unsullied dignity. Her appeal to posterity is one against the injustice of those who committed such crimes in the name of Liberty. She makes it in behalf of herself and her husband. I would put beside it, on the shelf, a little volume, containing a similar appeal from the verdict of contemporaries to that of mankind, made by Godwin in behalf of his wife, the celebrated, the by most men detested, Mary Wolstonecraft. In his view, it was an appeal from the injustice of those who did such wrong in the name of virtue. Were this little book interesting for no other cause, it would be so for the generous affection evinced under the peculiar circumstances. This man had courage to love and honor this woman in the face of the world's sentence, and of all that was repulsive in her own past history. He believed he saw of what soul she was, and that the impulses she had struggled to act out were noble, though the opinions to which they had led might not be thoroughly weighed. He loved her, and he defended her for the meaning and tendency of her inner life. It was a good fact.

Mary Wolstonecraft, like Madame Dudevant (commonly known as George Sand) in our day, was a woman whose existence better proved the need of some new interpretation of Woman's Rights than anything she wrote. Such beings as these, rich in genius, of most tender sympathies, capable of high virtue and a chastened harmony, ought not to find themselves, by birth, in a place so narrow, that, in breaking bonds, they become outlaws. Were there as much room in the world for such, as in Spenser's poem for Britomart, they would not run their heads so wildly against the walls, but prize their shelter rather. They find their way, at last, to light and air, but the world will not take off the brand it has set upon them. The champion of the Rights of Woman found, in Godwin, one who would plead that cause like a brother. He who delineated with such purity of traits the form of Woman in the Marguerite, of whom the weak St. Leon could never learn to be worthy, — a pearl indeed whose price was above rubies, — was not false in life to the faith by which he had hallowed his romance. He acted, as he wrote, like a brother. This form of appeal rarely fails to touch the basest man : — " Are you acting toward other women in the way you would have men act towards your sister?" George Sand smokes, wears male attire, wishes to be addressed as " Mon frère ; " —

perhaps, if she found those who were as brothers indeed, she would not care whether she were brother or sister.* We rejoice to see that she, who expresses such a painful contempt for men in most of her works, as shows she must have known great wrong from them, depicts, in " La Roche Mauprat," a man raised by the workings of love from the depths of savage sensualism to a moral and intellectual life.   It was love for a pure object, for a steadfast woman, one of those who, the Italian said, could make the " stair to heaven."

This author, beginning like the many in assault upon bad institutions, and external ills, yet deepening the experience through comparative freedom, sees at last that the only efficient remedy must come from individual character.   These bad institutions, indeed, it may always be replied, prevent individuals from forming good character, therefore we must remove them.   Agreed; yet keep steadily the higher aim in view.   Could you clear away all the bad forms of society, it is vain, unless the individual begin to be ready for better.   There must be a parallel movement in these two branches of life.   And all the rules left by Moses availed less to further the best life than the living example of one Messiah.

Still the mind of the age struggles confusedly with these problems, better discerning as yet the ill it can no longer bear, than the good by which it may super-

* A note appended by my sister in this place, in the first edition, is here omitted, because it is incorporated in another article in this volume, treating of George Sand more at length. — [ED.]

sede it. But women like Sand will speak now and cannot be silenced; their characters and their eloquence alike foretell an era when such as they shall easier learn to lead true lives. But though such forebode, not such shall be parents of it.* Those who would reform the world must show that they do not speak in the heat of wild impulse; their lives must be unstained by passionate error; they must be severe lawgivers to themselves. They must be religious students of the divine purpose with regard to man, if they would not confound the fancies of a day with the requisitions of eternal good. Their liberty must be the liberty of law and knowledge. But as to the transgressions against custom which have caused such outcry against those of noble intention, it may be observed that the resolve of Eloisa to be only the mistress of Abelard, was that of one who saw in practice around her the contract of marriage made the seal of degradation. Shelley feared not to be fettered, unless so to be was to be false. Wherever abuses are seen, the timid will suffer; the bold will protest. But society has a right to outlaw them till she has revised her law; and this she must be taught to do, by one who speaks with authority, not in anger or haste.

If Godwin's choice of the calumniated authoress of the " Rights of Woman," for his honored wife, be a sign of a new era, no less so is an article to which I have alluded some pages back, published five or six years ago in one of the English Reviews, where the writer, in doing full justice to Eloisa, shows his bitter regret that she lives not

*Appendix E.

now to love him, who might have known better how to prize her love than did the egotistical Abelard.

These marriages, these characters, with all their imperfections, express an onward tendency. They speak of aspiration of soul, of energy of mind, seeking clearness and freedom. Of a like promise are the tracts lately published by Goodwyn Barmby (the European Pariah, as he calls himself) and his wife Catharine. Whatever we may think of their measures, we see in them wedlock; the two minds are wed by the only contract that can permanently avail, that of a common faith and a common purpose.

We might mention instances, nearer home, of minds, partners in work and in life, sharing together, on equal terms, public and private interests, and which wear not, on any side, the aspect of offence shown by those lastnamed: persons who steer straight onward, yet, in our comparatively free life, have not been obliged to run their heads against any wall. But the principles which guide them might, under petrified and oppressive institutions, have made them warlike, paradoxical, and, in some sense, Pariahs. The phenomena are different, the law is the same, in all these cases. Men and women have been obliged to build up their house anew from the very foundation. If they found stone ready in the quarry, they took it peaceably; otherwise they alarmed the country by pulling down old towers to get materials.

These are all instances of marriage as intellectual companionship. The parties meet mind to mind, and a mutual trust is produced, which can buckler them against a million. They work together for a common purpose, and, in all these instances, with the same implement, — the pen. The pen and the writing-desk furnish forth as naturally the retirement of Woman as of Man.

A pleasing expression, in this kind, is afforded by the union in the names of the Howitts. William and Mary Howitt we heard named together for years, supposing them to be brother and sister; the equality of labors and reputation, even so, was auspicious; more so, now we find them man and wife. In his late work on Germany, Howitt mentions his wife, with pride, as one among the constellation of distinguished English-women, and in a graceful, simple manner. And still we contemplate with pleasure the partnership in literature and affection between the Howitts,— the congenial pursuits and productions — the pedestrian tours wherein the married pair showed that marriage, on a wide enough basis, does not destroy the "inexhaustible" entertainment which lovers find in one another's company.

In naming these instances, I do not mean to imply that community of employment is essential to the union of husband and wife, more than to the union of friends. Harmony exists in difference, no less than in likeness, if only the same key-note govern both parts. Woman the poem, Man the poet! Woman the heart, Man the head! Such divisions are only important when they are never to be transcended. If nature is never bound down, nor the voice of inspiration stifled, that is enough. We are pleased that women should write and speak, if they feel need of it, from having something to tell; but silence for ages would be no misfortune, if that silence be from divine command, and not from Man's tradition.

While Goetz Von Berlichingen rides to battle, his wife is busy in the kitchen; but difference of occupation does not prevent that community of inward life, that perfect esteem, with which he says,

"Whom God loves, to him gives he such a wife."

Manzoni thus dedicates his "Adelchi."

"To his beloved and venerated wife, Enrichetta Luigia Blondel, who, with conjugal affection and maternal wisdom, has preserved a virgin mind, the author dedicates this 'Adelchi,' grieving that he could not, by a more splendid and more durable monument, honor the dear name, and the memory of so many virtues."

The relation could not be fairer, nor more equal, if she, too, had written poems. Yet the position of the parties might have been the reverse as well; the Woman might have sung the deeds, given voice to the life of the Man, and beauty would have been the result; as we see, in pictures of Arcadia, the nymph singing to the shepherds, or the shepherd, with his pipe, alluring the nymphs; either makes a good picture. The sounding lyre requires not muscular strength, but energy of soul to animate the hand which would control it. Nature seems to delight in varying the arrangements, as if to show that she will be fettered by no rule; and we must admit the same varieties that she admits.

The fourth and highest grade of marriage union is the religious, which may be expressed as pilgrimage toward a common shrine. This includes the others: home sympathies and household wisdom, for these pilgrims must know how to assist each other along the dusty way; intellectual communion, for how sad it would be on such a journey to have a companion to whom you could not communicate your thoughts and aspirations as they sprang to life; who would have no feeling for the prospects that open, more and more glorious as we advance; who would never see the flowers that may be gathered by the most industrious traveller! It must include all these.

Such a fellow-pilgrim Count Zinzendorf seems to have found in his countess, of whom he thus writes:

"Twenty-five years' experience has shown me that just the help-meet whom I have is the only one that could suit my vocation. Who else could have so carried through my family affairs? Who lived so spotlessly before the world? Who so wisely aided me in my rejection of a dry morality? Who so clearly set aside the Pharisaism which, as years passed, threatened to creep in among us? Who so deeply discerned as to the spirits of delusion which sought to bewilder us? Who would have governed my whole economy so wisely, richly and hospitably, when circumstances commanded? Who have taken indifferently the part of servant or mistress, without, on the one side, affecting an especial spirituality; on the other, being sullied by any worldly pride? Who, in a community where all ranks are eager to be on a level, would, from wise and real causes, have known how to maintain inward and outward distinctions? Who, without a murmur, have seen her husband encounter such dangers by land and sea? Who undertaken with him, and *sustained*, such astonishing pilgrimages? Who, amid such difficulties, would have always held up her head and supported me? Who found such vast sums of money, and acquitted them on her own credit? And, finally, who, of all human beings, could so well understand and interpret to others my inner and outer being as this one, of such nobleness in her way of thinking, such great intellectual capacity, and so free from the theological perplexities that enveloped me ! ' "

Let any one peruse, with all intentness, the lineaments of this portrait, and see if the husband had not reason, with this air of solemn rapture and conviction, to challenge comparison? We are reminded of the majestic cadence of the line whose feet step in the just proportion of Humanity,

" Daughter of God and Man, accomplished Eve ! "

An observer* adds this testimony :

" We may, in many marriages, regard it as the best arrangement, if the man has so much advantage over his wife, that she can, without much thought of her own, be led and directed by him as by a father. But it was not so with the count and his consort. She was not made to be a copy; she was an original; and, while she loved and honored him, she thought for herself, on all subjects, with so much intelligence, that he could and did look on her as a sister and friend also."

Compare with this refined specimen of a religiously

* Spangenberg.

civilized life the following imperfect sketch of a North
American Indian, and we shall see that the same causes
will always produce the same results. The Flying
Pigeon (Ratchewaine) was the wife of a barbarous chief,
who had six others; but she was his only true wife,
because the only one of a strong and pure character, and,
having this, inspired a veneration, as like as the mind of
the man permitted to that inspired by the Countess Zinzendorf. She died when her son was only four years
old, yet left on his mind a feeling of reverent love worthy
the thought of Christian chivalry. Grown to manhood,
he shed tears on seeing her portrait.

THE FLYING PIGEON.

" Ratchewaine was chaste, mild, gentle in her disposition, kind, generous, and devoted to her husband. A
harsh word was never known to proceed from her mouth;
nor was she ever known to be in a passion. Mahaskah
used to say of her, after her death, that her hand was
shut when those who did not want came into her presence; but when the really poor came in, it was like a
strainer full of holes, letting all she held in it pass
through. In the exercise of generous feeling she was
uniform. It was not indebted for its exercise to whim,
nor caprice, nor partiality. No matter of what nation
the applicant for her bounty was, or whether at war or
peace with her nation; if he were hungry, she fed him;
if naked, she clothed him; and, if houseless, she gave
him shelter. The continued exercise of this generous
feeling kept her poor. And she has been known to give

away her last blanket — all the honey that was in the lodge, the last bladder of bear's oil, and the last piece of dried meat.

" She was scrupulously exact in the observance of all the religious rites which her faith imposed upon her. Her conscience is represented to have been extremely tender. She often feared that her acts were displeasing to the Great Spirit, when she would blacken her face, and retire to some lone place, and fast and pray."

To these traits should be added, but for want of room, anecdotes which show the quick decision and vivacity of her mind. Her face was in harmony with this combination. Her brow is as ideal and the eyes and lids as devout and modest as the Italian picture of the Madonna, while the lower part of the face has the simplicity and childish strength of the Indian race. Her picture presents the finest specimen of Indian beauty we have ever seen. Such a Woman is the sister and friend of all beings, as the worthy Man is their brother and helper.

With like pleasure we survey the pairs wedded on the eve of missionary effort. They, indeed, are fellow-pilgrims on the well-made road, and whether or no they accomplish all they hope for the sad Hindoo, or the nearer savage, we feel that in the burning waste their love is like to be a healing dew, in the forlorn jungle a tent of solace to one another. They meet, as children of one Father, to read together one book of instruction.

We must insert in this connection the most beautiful picture presented by ancient literature of wedded love under this noble form.

It is from the romance in which Xenophon, the chivalrous Greek, presents his ideal of what human nature should be.

The generals of Cyrus had taken captive a princess, a woman of unequalled beauty, and hastened to present her to the prince as that part of the spoil he would think most worthy of his acceptance. Cyrus visits the lady, and is filled with immediate admiration by the modesty and majesty with which she receives him. He finds her name is Panthea, and that she is the wife of Abradatus, a young king whom she entirely loves. He protects her as a sister, in his camp, till he can restore her to her husband.

After the first transports of joy at this reünion, the heart of Panthea is bent on showing her love and gratitude to her magnanimous and delicate protector. And as she has nothing so precious to give as the aid of Abradatus, that is what she most wishes to offer. Her husband is of one soul with her in this, as in all things.

The description of her grief and self-destruction, after the death which ensued upon this devotion, I have seen quoted, but never that of their parting when she sends him forth to battle. I shall copy both. If they have been read. by any of my readers, they may be so again with profit in this connection, for never were the heroism of a true Woman, and the purity of love in a true marriage, painted in colors more delicate and more lively.

" The chariot of Abradatus, that had four perches and eight horses, was completely adorned for him; and when he was going to put on his linen corslet, which was a sort

of armor used by those of his country, Panthea brought
him a golden helmet, and arm-pieces, broad bracelets for
his wrists, a purple habit that reached down to his feet,
and hung in folds at the bottom, and a crest dyed of a
violet color. These things she had made, unknown to
her husband, and by taking the measure of his armor.
He wondered when he saw them, and inquired thus of
Panthea : ' And have you made me these arms, woman,
by destroying your own ornaments ? '   ' No, by Jove ! '
said Panthea, ' not what is the most valuable of them ;
for it is you, if you appear to others to be what I think
you, that will be my greatest ornament.'   And, saying
that, she put on him the armor, and, though she endeav-
ored to conceal it, the tears poured down her cheeks.
When Abradatus, who was before a man of fine appearance, was set out in those arms, he appeared the most
beautiful and noble of all, especially being likewise so by
nature.   Then, taking the reins from the driver, he was
just preparing to mount the chariot, when Panthea, after
she had desired all that were there to retire, thus said :

" ' O Abradatus ! if ever there was a woman who had a
greater regard to her husband than to her own soul, I
believe you know that I am such an one ; what need I
therefore speak of things in particular ? for I reckon that
my actions have convinced you more than any words I
can now use.   And yet, though I stand thus affected
toward you, as you know I do, I swear, by this friendship
of mine and yours, that I certainly would rather choose
to be put under ground jointly with you, approving yourself a brave man, than to live with you in disgrace and

shame; so much do I think you and myself worthy of the noblest things. Then I think that we both lie under great obligations to Cyrus, that, when I was a captive, and chosen out for himself, he thought fit to treat me neither as a slave, nor, indeed, as a woman of mean account, but he took and kept me for you, as if I were his brother's wife. Besides, when Araspes, who was my guard, went away from him, I promised him, that, if he would allow me to send for you, you would come to him, and approve yourself a much better and more faithful friend than Araspes.'

"Thus she spoke; and Abradatus, being struck with admiration at her discourse, laying his hand gently on her head, and lifting up his eyes to heaven, made this prayer: 'Do thou, O greatest Jove! grant me to appear a husband worthy of Panthea, and a friend worthy of Cyrus, who has done us so much honor!'

"Having said this, he mounted the chariot by the door of the driver's seat; and, after he had got up, when the driver shut the door, Panthea, who had now no other way to salute him, kissed the seat of the chariot. The chariot then moved, and she, unknown to him, followed, till Abradatus turning about, and seeing her, said: 'Take courage, Panthea! Fare you happily and well, and now go your ways.' On this her women and servants carried her to her conveyance, and, laying her down, concealed her by throwing the covering of a tent over her. The people, though Abradatus and his chariot made a noble spectacle, were not able to look at him till Panthea was gone."

After the battle —

" Cyrus calling to some of his servants, ' Tell me, said
he, ' has any one seen Abradatus? for I admire that he
now does not appear.'   One replied, ' My sovereign, it is
because he is not living, but died in the battle as he broke
in with his chariot on the Egyptians.   All the rest, except his particular companions, they say, turned off when
they saw the Egyptians' compact body.   His wife is now
said to have taken up his dead body, to have placed it
in the carriage that she herself was conveyed in, and to
have brought it hither to some place on the river Pactolus,
and her servants are digging a grave on a certain elevation.   They say that his wife, after setting him out with
all the ornaments she has, is sitting on the ground with
his head on her knees.'   Cyrus, hearing this, gave himself a blow on the thigh, mounted his horse at a leap, and,
taking with him a thousand horse, rode away to this scene
of affliction ; but gave orders to Gadatas and Gobryas to
take with them all the rich ornaments proper for a friend
and an excellent man deceased, and to follow after him ;
and whoever had herds of cattle with him, he ordered
them to take both oxen, and horses, and sheep in good
number, and to bring them away to the place where, by
inquiry, they should find him to be, that he might sacrifice these to Abradatus.

" As soon as he saw the woman sitting on the ground,
and the dead body there lying, he shed tears at the
afflicting sight, and said : ' Alas ! thou brave and faithful
soul, hast thou left us, and art thou gone ? '   At the
same time he took him by the right hand, and the hand

of the deceased came away, for it had been cut off with a
sword by the Egyptians. He, at the sight of this, became
yet much more concerned than before. The woman
shrieked out in a lamentable manner, and, taking the
hand from Cyrus, kissed it, fitted it to its proper place
again, as well as she could, and said: 'The rest, Cyrus,
is in the same condition, but what need you see it?
And I know that I was not one of the least concerned in
these his sufferings, and, perhaps, you were not less so;
for I, fool that I was! frequently exhorted him to behave
in such a manner as to appear a friend to you, worthy of
notice; and I know he never thought of what he himself
should suffer, but of what he should do to please you.
He is dead, therefore,' said she, ' without reproach, and I,
who urged him on, sit here alive.' Cyrus, shedding tears
for some time in silence, then spoke : —' He has died,
woman, the noblest death; for he has died victorious!
Do you adorn him with these things that I furnish you
with.' (Gobryas and Gadatas were then come up, and
had brought rich ornaments in great abundance with
them.) 'Then,' said he, 'be assured that he shall not
want respect and honor in all other things; but, over
and above, multitudes shall concur in raising him a
monument that shall be worthy of us, and all the sacrifices shall be made him that are proper to be made in
honor of a brave man. You shall not be left destitute,
but, for the sake of your modesty and every other virtue,
I will pay you all other honors, as well as place those
about you who will conduct you wherever you please.
Do you but make it known to me where it is that you

desire to be conveyed to.'   And Panthea replied : ' Be
confident, Cyrus, I will not conceal from you to whom
it is that I desire to go.'

" He, having said this, went away with great pity for
her that she should have lost such a husband, and for
the man that he should have left such a wife behind him,
never to see her more.   Panthea then gave orders for her
servants to retire, ' till such time,' said she, ' as I shall
have lamented my husband as I please.'   Her nurse she
bid to stay, and gave orders that, when she was dead,
she would wrap her and her husband up in one mantle
together.   The nurse, after having repeatedly begged her
not to do this, and meeting with no success, but observing
her to grow angry, sat herself down, breaking out into
tears.   She, being beforehand provided with a sword,
killed herself, and, laying her head down on her husband's breast, she died.   The nurse set up a lamentable
cry, and covered them both, as Panthea had directed.

" Cyrus, as soon as he was informed of what the woman
had done, being struck with it, went to help her if he
could.   The servants, three in number, seeing what had
been done, drew their swords and killed themselves, as
they stood at the place where she had ordered them.
And the monument is now said to have been raised by
continuing the mound on to the servants ; and on a pillar
above, they say, the names of the man and woman were
written in Syriac letters.

" Below were three pillars, and they were inscribed
thus, ' Of the servants.'   Cyrus, when he came to this
melancholy scene, was struck with admiration of the

woman, and, having lamented over her, went away. He took care, as was proper, that all the funeral rites should be paid them in the noblest manner, and the monument, they say, was raised up to a very great size."

———

These be the ancients, who, so many assert, had no idea of the dignity of Woman, or of marriage. Such love Xenophon could paint as subsisting between those who after death "would see one another never more." Thousands of years have passed since, and with the reception of the Cross, the nations assume the belief that those who part thus may meet again and forever, if spiritually fitted to one another, as Abradatus and Panthea were, and yet do we see such marriages among them? If at all, how often?

I must quote two more short passages from Xenophon, for he is a writer who pleases me well.

Cyrus, receiving the Armenians whom he had conquered —

" 'Tigranes,' said he, 'at what rate would you purchase the regaining of your wife?' Now Tigranes happened to be *but lately married*, and had a very great love for his wife." (That clause perhaps sounds *modern*.)

" ' Cyrus,' said he, 'I would ransom her at the expense of my life.'

" 'Take then your own to yourself,' said he. * * *

" When they came home, one talked of Cyrus' wisdom, another of his patience and resolution, another of his mildness. One spoke of his beauty and smallness of his person, and, on that, Tigranes asked his wife, 'And

do you, Armenian dame, think Cyrus handsome?'
'Truly,' said she, 'I did not look at him.' 'At
whom, then, *did* you look?' said Tigranes. 'At him
who said that, to save me from servitude, he would ransom me at the expense of his own life.' "

From the Banquet. —

"Socrates, who observed her with pleasure, said, 'This
young girl has confirmed me in the opinion I have had,
for a long time, that the female sex are nothing inferior
to ours, excepting only in strength of body, or, perhaps,
in steadiness of judgment.' "

In the Economics, the manner in which the husband
gives counsel to his young wife presents the model of
politeness and refinement. Xenophon is thoroughly the
gentleman; gentle in breeding and in soul. All the men
he describes are so, while the shades of manner are distinctly marked. There is the serene dignity of Socrates,
with gleams of playfulness thrown across its cool, religious
shades, the princely mildness of Cyrus, and the more
domestic elegance of the husband in the Economics.

There is no way that men sin more against refinement,
as well as discretion, than in their conduct toward their
wives. Let them look at the men of Xenophon. Such
would know how to give counsel, for they would know how
to receive it. They would feel that the most intimate
relations claimed most, not least, of refined courtesy.
They would not suppose that confidence justified carelessness, nor the reality of affection want of delicacy in the
expression of it.

Such men would be too wise to hide their affairs from the wife, and then expect her to act as if she knew them. They would know that, if she is expected to face calamity with courage, she must be instructed and trusted in prosperity, or, if they had failed in wise confidence, such as the husband shows in the Economics, they would be ashamed of anger or querulous surprise at the results that naturally follow.

Such men would not be exposed to the bad influence of bad wives; for all wives, bad or good, loved or unloved, inevitably influence their husbands, from the power their position not merely gives, but necessitates, of coloring evidence and infusing feelings in hours when the — patient, shall I call him? — is off his guard. Those who understand the wife's mind, and think it worth while to respect her springs of action, know better where they are. But to the bad or thoughtless man, who lives carelessly and irreverently so near another mind, the wrong he does daily back upon himself recoils. A Cyrus, an Abradatus, knows where he stands.

———

But to return to the thread of my subject.

Another sign of the times is furnished by the triumphs of Female Authorship. These have been great, and are constantly increasing. Women have taken possession of so many provinces for which men had pronounced them unfit, that, though these still declare there are some inaccessible to them, it is difficult to say just *where* they must stop.

The shining names of famous women have cast light upon the path of the sex, and many obstructions have been removed. When a Montague could learn better than her brother, and use her lore afterwards to such purpose as an observer, it seemed amiss to hinder women from preparing themselves to see, or from seeing all they could, when prepared. Since Somerville has achieved so much, will any young girl be prevented from seeking a knowledge of the physical sciences, if she wishes it? De Stael's name was not so clear of offence; she could not forget the Woman in the thought; while she was instructing you as a mind, she wished to be admired as a Woman; sentimental tears often dimmed the eagle glance. Her intellect, too, with all its splendor, trained in a drawing-room, fed on flattery, was tainted and flawed; yet its beams make the obscurest school-house in New England warmer and lighter to the little rugged girls who are gathered together on its wooden bench. They may never through life hear her name, but she is not the less their benefactress.

The influence has been such, that the aim certainly is, now, in arranging school instruction for girls, to give them as fair a field as boys. As yet, indeed, these arrangements are made with little judgment or reflection; just as the tutors of Lady Jane Grey, and other distinguished women of her time, taught them Latin and Greek, because they knew nothing else themselves, so now the improvement in the education of girls is to be made by giving them young men as teachers, who only teach what has been taught themselves at college, while methods and topics need revision for these new subjects, which could better be made by those who had experienced the same wants. Women are, often, at the head of these institutions; but they have, as yet, seldom been thinking women, capable of organizing a new whole for the wants of the time, and choosing persons to officiate in the departments. And when some portion of instruction of a good sort is got from the school, the far greater proportion which is infused from the general atmosphere of society contradicts its purport. Yet books and a little elementary instruction are not furnished in vain. Women are better aware how great and rich the universe is, not so easily blinded by narrowness or partial views of a home circle. " Her mother did so before her " is no longer a sufficient excuse. Indeed, it was never received as an excuse to mitigate the severity of censure, but was adduced as a reason, rather, why there should be no effort made for reformation.

Whether much or little has been done, or will be done, — whether women will add to the talent of narration the power of systematizing, — whether they will carve marble, as well as draw and paint, — is not important. But that it should be acknowledged that they have intellect which needs developing — that they should not be considered complete, if beings of affection and habit alone — is important.

Yet even this acknowledgment, rather conquered by Woman than proffered by Man, has been sullied by the usual selfishness. Too much is said of women being better educated, that they may become better companions and mothers *for men.* They should be fit for such companionship, and we have mentioned, with satisfaction, in-

stances where it has been established.   Earth knows no
fairer, holier relation than that of a mother.   It is one
which, rightly understood, must both promote and
require the highest attainments.   But a being of infinite
scope must not be treated with an exclusive view to any
one relation.   Give the soul free course, let the organization, both of body and mind, be freely developed, and
the being will be fit for any and every relation to which
it may be called.   The intellect, no more than the sense
of hearing, is to be cultivated merely that Woman may be
a more valuable companion to Man, but because the Power
who gave a power, by its mere existence signifies that it
must be brought out toward perfection.

In this regard of self-dependence, and a greater simplicity and fulness of being, we must hail as a prelimi-
nary the increase of the class contemptuously designated
as " old maids."

We cannot wonder at the aversion with which old
bachelors and old maids have been regarded.   Marriage
is the natural means of forming a sphere, of taking root
in the earth ; it requires more strength to do this without
such an opening ; very many have failed, and their imperfections have been in every one's way.   They have
been more partial, more harsh, more officious and imper-
tinent, than those compelled by severer friction to render
themselves endurable.   Those who have a more full experience of the instincts have a distrust as to whether the
unmarried can be thoroughly human and humane, such as
is hinted in the saying, " Old maids' and bachelors' chil-

dren are well cared for," which derides at once their ignorance and their presumption.

Yet the business of society has become so complex, that it could now scarcely be carried on without the presence of these despised auxiliaries; and detachments from the army of aunts and uncles are wanted to stop gaps in every hedge. They rove about, mental and moral Ishmaelites, pitching their tents amid the fixed and ornamented homes of men.

In a striking variety of forms, genius of late, both at home and abroad, has paid its tribute to the character of the Aunt and the Uncle, recognizing in these personages the spiritual parents, who have supplied defects in the treatment of the busy or careless actual parents.

They also gain a wider, if not so deep experience. Those who are not intimately and permanently linked with others, are thrown upon themselves; and, if they do not there find peace and incessant life, there is none to flatter them that they are not very poor, and very mean.

A position which so constantly admonishes, may be of inestimable benefit. The person may gain, undistracted by other relationships, a closer communion with the one. Such a use is made of it by saints and sibyls. Or she may be one of the lay sisters of charity, a canoness, bound by an inward vow, — or the useful drudge of all men, the Martha, much sought, little prized, — or the intellectual interpreter of the varied life she sees; the Urania of a half-formed world's twilight.

Or she may combine all these. Not " needing to

care that she may please a husband," a frail and limited
being, her thoughts may turn to the centre, and she may,
by steadfast contemplation entering into the secret of
truth and love, use it for the good of all men, instead of a
chosen few, and interpret through it all the forms of life.
It is possible, perhaps, to be at once a priestly servant
and a loving muse.

Saints and geniuses have often chosen a lonely position,
in the faith that if, undisturbed by the pressure of near
ties, they would give themselves up to the inspiring spirit,
it would enable them to understand and reproduce life
better than actual experience could.

How many "old maids" take this high stand we cannot
say : it is an unhappy fact that too many who have come
before the eye are gossips rather, and not always good-
natured gossips. But if these abuse, and none make the
best of their vocation, yet it has not failed to produce
some good results. It has been seen by others, if not by
themselves, that beings, likely to be left alone, need to
be fortified and furnished within themselves ; and education and thought have tended more and more to regard
these beings as related to absolute Being, as well as to
others. It has been seen that, as the breaking of no
bond ought to destroy a man, so ought the missing of
none to hinder him from growing. And thus a circumstance of the time, which springs rather from its luxury
than its purity, has helped to place women on the true
platform.

Perhaps the next generation, looking deeper into this
matter, will find that contempt is put upon old maids, or

old women, at all, merely because they do not use the elixir which would keep them always young. Under its influence, a gem brightens yearly which is only seen to more advantage through the fissures Time makes in the casket.* No one thinks of Michael Angelo's Persican Sibyl, or St. Theresa, or Tasso's Leonora, or the Greek Electra, as an old maid, more than of Michael Angelo or Canova as old bachelors, though all had reached the period in life's course appointed to take that degree.

See a common woman at forty; scarcely has she the remains of beauty, of any soft poetic grace which gave her attraction as Woman, which kindled the hearts of those who looked on her to sparkling thoughts, or diffused round her a roseate air of gentle love. See her, who was, indeed, a lovely girl, in the coarse, full-blown dahlia flower of what is commonly matron-beauty, "fat, fair, and forty," showily dressed, and with manners as broad and full as her frill or satin cloak. People observe, "How well she is preserved!" "She is a fine woman still," they say. This woman, whether as a duchess in diamonds, or one of our city dames in mosaics, charms the poet's heart no more, and would look much out of place kneeling before the Madonna. She "does well the honors of her house," — "leads society," — is, in short, always spoken and thought of upholstery-wise.

Or see that care-worn face, from which every soft line is blotted,— those faded eyes, from which lonely tears have driven the flashes of fancy, the mild white beam of

* Appendix F.

a tender enthusiasm. This woman is not so ornamental
to a tea-party; yet she would please better, in picture.
Yet surely she, no more than the other, looks as a human
being should at the end of forty years. Forty years!
have they bound those brows with no garland? shed in
the lamp no drop of ambrosial oil?

Not so looked the Iphigenia in Aulis.* Her forty
years had seen her in anguish, in sacrifice, in utter loneliness. But those pains were borne for her father and
her country; the sacrifice she had made pure for herself
and those around her. Wandering alone at night in the
vestal solitude of her imprisoning grove, she has looked
up through its " living summits " to the stars, which shed
down into her aspect their own lofty melody. At forty
she would not misbecome the marble.

Not so looks the Persica. She is withered; she is
faded; the drapery that enfolds her has in its dignity an
angularity, too, that tells of age, of sorrow, of a stern
resignation to the *must*. But her eye, that torch of the
soul, is untamed, and, in the intensity of her reading, we
see a soul invincibly young in faith and hope. Her age
is her charm, for it is the night of the past that gives
this beacon-fire leave to shine. Wither more and more,
black Chrysalid! thou dost but give the winged beauty
time to mature its splendors!

Not so looked Victoria Colonna, after her life of a
great hope, and of true conjugal fidelity. She had been,
not merely a bride, but a wife, and each hour had helped
to plume the noble bird. A coronet of pearls will not

* Appendix G

shame her brow; it is white and ample, a worthy altar
for love and thought.

Even among the North American Indians, a race of
men as completely engaged in mere instinctive life as
almost any in the world, and where each chief, keeping
many wives as useful servants, of course looks with no
kind eye on celibacy in Woman, it was excused in the following instance mentioned by Mrs. Jameson. A woman
dreamt in youth that she was betrothed to the Sun. She
built her a wigwam apart, filled it with emblems of her
alliance, and means of an independent life. There she
passed her days, sustained by her own exertions, and true
to her supposed engagement.

In any tribe, we believe, a woman, who lived as if she
was betrothed to the Sun, would be tolerated, and the
rays which made her youth blossom sweetly, would crown
her with a halo in age.

There is, on this subject, a nobler view than hereto-
fore, if not the noblest, and improvement here must coin-
cide with that in the view taken of marriage. "We must
have units before we can have union," says one of the ripe
thinkers of the times.

If larger intellectual resources begin to be deemed
needful to Woman, still more is a spiritual dignity in her,
or even the mere assumption of it, looked upon with
respect. Joanna Southcote and Mother Anne Lee are
sure of a band of disciples; Ecstatica, Dolorosa, of en-
raptured believers who will visit them in their lowly huts,
and wait for days to revere them in their trances. The
foreign noble traverses land and sea to hear a few words

from the lips of the lowly peasant girl, whom he believes especially visited by the Most High.   Very beautiful, in this way, was the influence of the invalid of St. Petersburg, as described by De Maistre.

Mysticism, which may be defined as the brooding soul of the world, cannot fail of its oracular promise as to Woman.   "The mothers,"   "The mother of all things," are expressions of thought which lead the mind towards this side of universal growth.   Whenever a mystical whisper was heard, from Behmen down to St. Simon, sprang up the thought, that, if it be true, as the legend says, that Humanity withers through a fault committed by and a curse laid upon Woman, through her pure child, or influence, shall the new Adam, the redemption, arise.   Innocence is to be replaced by virtue, dependence by a willing submission, in the heart of the Virgin-Mother of the new race.

The spiritual tendency is toward the elevation of Woman, but the intellectual by itself is not so.   Plato sometimes seems penetrated by that high idea of love, which considers Man and Woman as the two-fold expression of one thought.   This the angel of Swedenborg, the angel of the coming age, cannot surpass, but only explain more fully.   But then again Plato, the man of intellect, treats Woman in the Republic as property, and, in the Timæus, says that Man, if he misuse the privileges of one life, shall be degraded into the form of Woman; and then, if he do not redeem himself, into that of a bird. This, as I said above, expresses most happily how anti-poetical is this state of mind.   For the poet, contemplating the world of things, selects various birds as the symbols of his most gracious and ethereal thoughts, just as he calls upon his genius as muse rather than as God. But the intellect, cold, is ever more masculine than feminine; warmed by emotion, it rushes toward mother-earth, and puts on the forms of beauty.

The electrical, the magnetic element in Woman has not been fairly brought out at any period. Everything might be expected from it; she has far more of it than Man. This is commonly expressed by saying that her intuitions are more rapid and more correct. You will often see men of high intellect absolutely stupid in regard to the atmospheric changes, the fine invisible links which connect the forms of life around them, while common women, if pure and modest, so that a vulgar self do not overshadow the mental eye, will seize and delineate these with unerring discrimination.

Women who combine this organization with creative genius are very commonly unhappy at present. They see too much to act in conformity with those around them, and their quick impulses seem folly to those who do not discern the motives. This is an usual effect of the apparition of genius, whether in Man or Woman, but is more frequent with regard to the latter, because a harmony, an obvious order and self-restraining decorum, is most expected from her.

Then women of genius, even more than men, are likely to be enslaved by an impassioned sensibility. The world repels them more rudely, and they are of weaker bodily frame.

Those who seem overladen with electricity frighten those around them.   " When she merely enters the room, I am what the French call *herissé*," said a man of petty feelings and worldly character of such a woman, whose depth of eye and powerful motion announced the conductor of the mysterious fluid.

Woe to such a woman who finds herself linked to such a man in bonds too close !   It is the cruelest of errors. He will detest her with all the bitterness of wounded self-love.   He will take the whole prejudice of manhood upon himself, and, to the utmost of his power, imprison and torture her by its imperious rigors.

Yet, allow room enough, and the electric fluid will be found to invigorate and embellish, not destroy life. Such women are the great actresses, the songsters. Such traits we read in a late searching, though too French, analysis of the character of Mademoiselle Rachel, by a modern La Rochefoucault.   The Greeks thus represent the muses ; they have not the golden serenity of Apollo ; they are *over*flowed with thought; there is something tragic in their air.   Such are the Sibyls of Guercino ; the eye is overfull of expression, dilated and lustrous ; it seems to have drawn the whole being into it.

Sickness is the frequent result of this overcharged existence.   To this region, however misunderstood, or interpreted with presumptuous carelessness, belong the phenomena of magnetism, or mesmerism, as it is now often called, where the trance of the Ecstatica purports to be produced by the agency of one human being on another, instead of, as in her case, direct from the spirit.

The worldling has his sneer at this as at the services of religion. "The churches can always be filled with women"—"Show me a man in one of your magnetic states, and I will believe."

Women are, indeed, the easy victims both of priest-craft and self-delusion; but this would not be, if the intellect was developed in proportion to the other powers. They would then have a regulator, and be more in equi-poise, yet must retain the same nervous susceptibility while their physical structure is such as it is.

It is with just that hope that we welcome everything that tends to strengthen the fibre and develop the nature on more sides. When the intellect and affections are in harmony; when intellectual consciousness is calm and deep; inspiration will not be confounded with fancy.

> Then, " she who advances
> With rapturous, lyrical glances,
> Singing the song of the earth, singing
> Its hymn to the Gods,"

will not be pitied as a mad-woman, nor shrunk from as unnatural.

The Greeks, who saw everything in forms, which we are trying to ascertain as law, and classify as cause, em-bodied all this in the form of Cassandra. Cassandra was only unfortunate in receiving her gift too soon. The remarks, however, that the world still makes in such cases, are well expressed by the Greek dramatist.

In the Trojan dames there are fine touches of nature with regard to Cassandra. Hecuba shows that mixture of shame and reverence that prosaic kindred always do

toward the inspired child, the poet, the elected sufferer for
the race.

When the herald announces that Cassandra is chosen
to be the mistress of Agamemnon, Hecuba answers, with
indignation, betraying the pride and faith she involun-
tarily felt in this daughter.

> "*Hec.* The maiden of Phoebus, to whom the golden-haired
>   Gave as a privilege a virgin life !
>
> *Tal.* Love of the inspired maiden hath pierced him.
>
> *Hec.* Then cast away, my child, the sacred keys, and from thy person
>   The consecrated garlands which thou wearest."

Yet, when, a moment after, Cassandra appears, singing, wildly, her inspired song, Hecuba calls her, "My
frantic child."

Yet how graceful she is in her tragic *raptus*, the
chorus shows.

> "*Chorus.* How sweetly at thy house's ills thou smil'st,
>   Chanting what, haply, thou wilt not show true."

If Hecuba dares not trust her highest instinct about
her daughter, still less can the vulgar mind of the herald
Talthybius, a man not without feeling, but with no
princely, no poetic blood, abide the wild, prophetic mood
which insults all his prejudices.

> "*Tal.* The venerable, and that accounted wise,
>   Is nothing better than that of no repute ;
>   For the greatest king of all the Greeks,
>   The dear son of Atreus, is possessed with the love
>   Of this mad-woman. I, indeed, am poor ;
>   Yet I would not receive her to my bed."

The royal Agamemnon could see the beauty of Cassandra ; *he* was not afraid of her prophetic gifts.

The best topic for a chapter on this subject, in the present day, would be the history of the Seeress of Prevorst, the best observed subject of magnetism in our present times, and who, like her ancestresses of Delphos, was roused to ecstasy or phrensy by the touch of the laurel.

I observe in her case, and in one known to me here, that what might have been a gradual and gentle disclosure of remarkable powers was broken and jarred into disease by an unsuitable marriage. Both these persons were unfortunate in not understanding what was involved in this relation, but acted ignorantly, as their friends desired. They thought that this was the inevitable destiny of Woman. But when engaged in the false position, it was impossible for them to endure its dissonances, as those of less delicate perceptions can ; and the fine flow of life was checked and sullied. They grew sick ; but, even so, learned and disclosed more than those in health are wont to do.

In such cases, worldlings sneer; but reverent men learn wondrous news, either from the person observed, or by thoughts caused in themselves by the observation. Fenelon learns from Guyon, Kerner from his Seeress, what we fain would know. But to appreciate such disclosures one must be a child; and here the phrase, " women and children," may, perhaps, be interpreted aright, that only little children shall enter into the kingdom of heaven.

All these motions of the time, tides that betoken a waxing moon, overflow upon our land. The world at large is readier to let Woman learn and manifest the capacities of her nature than it ever was before, and here is a less encumbered field and freer air than anywhere else. And it ought to be so ; we ought to pay for Isabella's jewels.

The names of nations are feminine — Religion, Virtue and Victory are feminine. To those who have a superstition, as to outward reigns, it is not without significance that the name of the queen of our mother-land should at this crisis be Victoria, — Victoria the First. Perhaps to us it may be given to disclose the era thus outwardly presaged.

Another Isabella too at this time ascends the throne. Might she open a new world to her sex ! But, probably, these poor little women are, least of any, educated to serve as examples or inspirers for the rest. The Spanish queen is younger ; we know of her that she sprained her foot the other day, dancing in her private apartments ; of Victoria, that she reads aloud, in a distinct voice and agreeable manner, her addresses to Parliament on certain solemn days, and, yearly, that she presents to the nation some new prop of royalty. These ladies have, very likely, been trained more completely to the puppet life than any other. The queens, who have been queens indeed, were trained by adverse circumstances to know the world around them and their own powers.

It is moving, while amusing, to read of the Scottish peasant measuring the print left by the queen's foot as she walks, and priding himself on its beauty. It is so natural to wish to find what is fair and precious in high places, — so astonishing to find the Bourbon a glutton, or the Guelph a dullard or gossip.

In our own country, women are, in many respects, better situated than men. Good books are allowed, with more time to read them. They are not so early forced into the bustle of life, nor so weighed down by demands for outward success. The perpetual changes, incident to our society, make the blood circulate freely through the body politic, and, if not favorable at present to the grace and bloom of life, they are so to activity, resource, and would be to reflection, but for a low materialist tendency, from which the women are generally exempt in themselves, though its existence, among the men, has a tendency to repress their impulses and make them doubt their instincts, thus often paralyzing their action during the best years.

But they have time to think, and no traditions chain them, and few conventionalities, compared with what must be met in other nations. There is no reason why they should not discover that the secrets of nature are open, the revelations of the spirit waiting, for whoever will seek them. When the mind is once awakened to this consciousness, it will not be restrained by the habits of the past, but fly to seek the seeds of a heavenly future.

Their employments are more favorable to meditation than those of men.

Woman is not addressed religiously here more than elsewhere. She is told that she should be worthy to be the mother of a Washington, or the companion of some good man. But in many, many instances, she has already learned that all bribes have the same flaw; that truth and good are to be sought solely for their own sakes. And, already, an ideal sweetness floats over many forms, shines in many eyes.

Already deep questions are put by young girls on the great theme : What shall I do to enter upon the eternal life ?

Men are very courteous to them. They praise them often, check them seldom. There is chivalry in the feeling toward "the ladies," which gives them the best seats in the stage-coach, frequent admission, not only to lectures of all sorts, but to courts of justice, halls of legislature, reform conventions. The newspaper editor "would be better pleased that the Lady's Book should be filled up exclusively by ladies. It would then, indeed, be a true gem, worthy to be presented by young men to the mistress of their affections." Can gallantry go further ?

In this country is venerated, wherever seen, the character which Goethe spoke of as an Ideal, which he saw actualized in his friend and patroness, the Grand Duchess Amelia : "The excellent woman is she, who, if the husband dies, can be a father to the children." And this, if read aright, tells a great deal.

Women who speak in public, if they have a moral power, such as has been felt from Angelina Grimke and Abby Kelly, — that is, if they speak for conscience' sake, to serve a cause which they hold sacred, — invariably subdue the prejudices of their hearers, and excite an interest proportionate to the aversion with which it had been the purpose to regard them.

A passage in a private letter so happily illustrates this, that it must be inserted here.

Abby Kelly in the Town-House of ————.

" The scene was not unheroic — to see that woman, true to humanity and her own nature, a centre of rude eyes and tongues, even gentlemen feeling licensed to make part of a species of mob around a female out of her sphere. As she took her seat in the desk amid the great noise, and in the throng, full, like a wave, of something to ensue, I saw her humanity in a gentleness and unpretension, tenderly open to the sphere around her, and, had she not been supported by the power of the will of genuineness and principle, she would have failed. It led her to prayer, which, in Woman especially, is childlike ; sensibility and will going to the side of God and looking up to him ; and humanity was poured out in aspiration.

" She acted like a gentle hero, with her mild decision and womanly calmness. All heroism is mild, and quiet, and gentle, for it is life and possession ; and combativeness and firmness show a want of actualness. She is as earnest, fresh and simple, as when she first entered the crusade. I think she did much good, more than the men in her place could do, for Woman feels more as being and reproducing — this brings the subject more into home relations. Men speak through, and mostly from intellect, and this addresses itself to that in others which is combative."

Not easily shall we find elsewhere, or before this time,

any written observations on the same subject, so delicate and profound.

The late Dr. Channing, whose enlarged and tender and religious nature shared every onward impulse of his time, though his thoughts followed his wishes with a deliberative caution which belonged to his habits and temperament, was greatly interested in these expectations for women. His own treatment of them was absolutely and thoroughly religious. He regarded them as souls, each of which had a destiny of its own, incalculable to other minds, and whose leading it must follow, guided by the light of a private conscience. He had sentiment, delicacy, kindness, taste; but they were all pervaded and ruled by this one thought, that all beings had souls, and must vindicate their own inheritance. Thus all beings were treated by him with an equal, and sweet, though solemn, courtesy. The young and unknown, the woman and the child, all felt themselves regarded with an infinite expectation, from which there was no reaction to vulgar prejudice. He demanded of all he met, to use his favorite phrase, "great truths."

His memory, every way dear and reverend, is, by many, especially cherished for this intercourse of unbroken respect.

At one time, when the progress of Harriet Martineau through this country, Angelina Grimke's appearance in public, and the visit of Mrs. Jameson, had turned his thoughts to this subject, he expressed high hopes as to what the coming era would bring to Woman. He had been much pleased with the dignified courage of Mrs.

Jameson in taking up the defence of her sex in a way
from which women usually shrink, because, if they express themselves on such subjects with sufficient force
and clearness to do any good, they are exposed to as-
saults whose vulgarity makes them painful. In intercourse with such a woman, he had shared her indignation
at the base injustice, in many respects, and in many
regions, done to the sex; and been led to think of it far
more than ever before. He seemed to think that he
might some time write upon the subject. That his aid is
withdrawn from the cause is a subject of great regret;
for, on this question as on others, he would have known
how to sum up the evidence, and take, in the noblest
spirit, middle ground. He always furnished a platform
on which opposing parties could stand and look at one
another under the influence of his mildness and enlightened candor.

Two younger thinkers, men both, have uttered noble
prophecies, auspicious for Woman. Kinmont, all whose
thoughts tended towards the establishment of the reign
of love and peace, thought that the inevitable means of
this would be an increased predominance given to the
idea of Woman. Had he lived longer, to see the growth
of the Peace Party, the reforms in life and medical practice which seek to substitute water for wine and drugs,
pulse for animal food, he would have been confirmed in
his view of the way in which the desired changes are to
be effected.

In this connection I must mention Shelley, who, like
all men of genius, shared the feminine development, and,

unlike many, knew it. His life was one of the first pulse-beats in the present reform-growth. He, too, abhorred blood and heat, and, by his system and his song, tended to reinstate a plant-like gentleness in the development of energy. In harmony with this, his ideas of marriage were lofty, and, of course, no less so of Woman, her nature, and destiny.

For Woman, if, by a sympathy as to outward condition, she is led to aid the enfranchisement of the slave, must be no less so, by inward tendency, to favor measures which promise to bring the world more thoroughly and deeply into harmony with her nature. When the lamb takes place of the lion as the emblem of nations, both women and men will be as children of one spirit, perpetual learners of the word and doers thereof, not hearers only.

A writer in the New York Pathfinder, in two articles headed "Femality," has uttered a still more pregnant word than any we have named. He views Woman truly from the soul, and not from society, and the depth and leading of his thoughts are proportionably remarkable. He views the feminine nature as a harmonizer of the vehement elements, and this has often been hinted elsewhere ; but what he expresses most forcibly is the lyrical, the inspiring and inspired apprehensiveness of her being.

This view being identical with what I have before attempted to indicate, as to her superior susceptibility to magnetic or electric influence, I will now try to express myself more fully.

There are two aspects of Woman's nature, represented by the ancients as Muse and Minerva. It is the former to which the writer in the Pathfinder looks. It is the latter which Wordsworth has in mind, when he says,

> "With a placid brow,
> Which woman ne'er should forfeit, keep thy vow."

The especial genius of Woman I believe to be electrical in movement, intuitive in function, spiritual in tendency. She excels not so easily in classification, or recreation, as in an instinctive seizure of causes, and a simple breathing out of what she receives, that has the singleness of life, rather than the selecting and energizing of art.

WOMAN AS MYSTIC

More native is it to her to be the living model of the artist than to set apart from herself any one form in objective reality; more native to inspire and receive the poem, than to create it. In so far as soul is in her completely developed, all soul is the same; but in so far as it is modified in her as Woman, it flows, it breathes, it sings, rather than deposits soil, or finishes work; and that which is especially feminine flushes, in blossom, the face of earth, and pervades, like air and water, all this seeming solid globe, daily renewing and purifying its life. Such may be the especially feminine element spoken of as Femality. But it is no more the order of nature that it should be incarnated pure in any form, than that the masculine energy should exist unmingled with it in any form.

Male and female represent the two sides of the great

MASCULINE
FEMININE
CONTINUUM

radical dualism.   But, in fact, they are perpetually passing into one another.   Fluid hardens to solid, solid rushes
to fluid.   There is no wholly masculine man, no purely
feminine woman.

History jeers at the attempts of physiologists to bind
great original laws by the forms which flow from them.
They make a rule; they say from observation what can
and cannot be.   In vain!   Nature provides exceptions
to every rule.   She sends women to battle, and sets
Hercules spinning; she enables women to bear immense
burdens, cold, and frost; she enables the man, who feels
maternal love, to nourish his infant like a mother.   Of
late she plays still gayer pranks.   Not only she de-
prives organizations, but organs, of a necessary end.   She
enables people to read with the top of the head, and see
with the pit of the stomach.   Presently she will make a
female Newton, and a male Syren.

Man partakes of the feminine in the Apollo, Woman
of the masculine as Minerva.

What I mean by the Muse is that unimpeded clearness
of the intuitive powers, which a perfectly truthful ad-
herence to every admonition of the higher instincts would
bring to a finely organized human being.   It may appear
as prophecy or as poesy.   It enabled Cassandra to fore-
see the results of actions passing round her; the Seeress
to behold the true character of the person through the
mask of his customary life.   (Sometimes she saw a feminine form behind the man, sometimes the reverse.)   It
enabled the daughter of Linnæus to see the soul of the

flower exhaling from the flower.*   It gave a man, but a poet-man, the power of which he thus speaks : " Often in my contemplation of nature, radiant intimations, and as it were sheaves of light, appear before me as to the facts of cosmogony, in which my mind has, perhaps, taken especial part." He wisely adds, " but it is necessary with earnestness to verify the knowledge we gain by these flashes of light." And none should forget this. Sight must be verified by light before it can deserve the honors of piety and genius.   Yet sight comes first, and of this sight of the world of causes, this approximation to the region of primitive motions, women I hold to be especially capable.   Even without equal freedom with the other sex, they have already shown themselves so ; and should these faculties have free play, I believe they will open new, deeper and purer sources of joyous inspiration than have as yet refreshed the earth.

Let us be wise, and not impede the soul.   Let her work as she will.   Let us have one creative energy, one incessant revelation.   Let it take what form it will, and let us not bind it by the past to man or woman, black or white.   Jove sprang from Rhea, Pallas from Jove.   So let it be.

If it has been the tendency of these remarks to call Woman rather to the Minerva side,—if I, unlike the

---

* The daughter of Linnaeus states, that, while looking steadfastly at the red lily, she saw its spirit hovering above it, as a red flame.   It is true, this, like many fair spirit-stories, may be explained away as an optical illusion, but its poetic beauty and meaning would, even then, make it valuable, as an illustration of the spiritual fact.

more generous writer, have spoken from society no less
than the soul,— let it be pardoned ! It is love that has
caused this,— love for many incarcerated souls, that
might be freed, could the idea of religious self-dependence be established in them, could the weakening habit
of dependence on others be broken up.

IDEAL OF SELF-
DEPENDENCE

Proclus teaches that every life has, in its sphere, a
totality or wholeness of the animating powers of the other
spheres ; having only, as its own characteristic, a predominance of some one power.   Thus Jupiter comprises,
within himself, the other twelve powers, which stand
thus : The first triad is *demiurgic or fabricative*, that is,
Jupiter, Neptune, Vulcan ; the second, *defensive*, Vesta,
Minerva, Mars ; the third, *vivific*, Ceres, Juno, Diana ;
and the fourth, Mercury, Venus, Apollo, *elevating and
harmonic*.   In the sphere of Jupiter, energy is predomi-
nant — with Venus, beauty ; but each comprehends and
apprehends all the others.

When the same community of life and consciousness of
mind begin among men, humanity will have, positively
and finally, subjugated its brute elements and Titanic
childhood ; criticism will have perished ; arbitrary limits
and ignorant censure be impossible ; all will have entered
upon the liberty of law, and the harmony of common
growth.

Then Apollo will sing to his lyre what Vulcan forges
on the anvil, and the Muse weave anew the tapestries of
Minerva.

It is, therefore, only in the present crisis that the preference is given to Minerva.   The power of continence

must establish the legitimacy of freedom, the power of self-poise the perfection of motion.

Every relation, every gradation of nature is incalculably precious, but only to the soul which is poised upon itself, and to whom no loss, no change, can bring dull discord, for it is in harmony with the central soul.

If any individual live too much in relations, so that he becomes a stranger to the resources of his own nature, he falls, after a while, into a distraction, or imbecility, from which he can only be cured by a time of isolation, which gives the renovating fountains time to rise up. With a society it is the same. Many minds, deprived of the traditionary or instinctive means of passing a cheerful existence, must find help in self-impulse, or perish. It is therefore that, while any elevation, in the view of union, is to be hailed with joy, we shall not decline celibacy as the great fact of the time. It is one from which no vow, no arrangement, can at present save a thinking mind. For now the rowers are pausing on their oars; they wait a change before they can pull together. All tends to illustrate the thought of a wise cotemporary. Union is only possible to those who are units. To be fit for relations in time, souls, whether of Man or Woman, must be able to do without them in the spirit.

It is therefore that I would have Woman lay aside all thought, such as she habitually cherishes, of being taught and led by men. I would have her, like the Indian girl, dedicate herself to the Sun, the Sun of Truth, and go nowhere if his beams did not make clear the path. I would have her free from compromise, from complaisance, from helplessness, because I would have her good enough and strong enough to love one and all beings, from the fulness, not the poverty of being.

Men, as at present instructed, will not help this work, because they also are under the slavery of habit. I have seen with delight their poetic impulses. A sister is the fairest ideal, and how nobly Wordsworth, and even Byron, have written of a sister!

There is no sweeter sight than to see a father with his little daughter. Very vulgar men become refined to the eye when leading a little girl by the hand. At that moment, the right relation between the sexes seems established, and you feel as if the man would aid in the noblest purpose, if you ask him in behalf of his little daughter. Once, two fine figures stood before me, thus. The father of very intellectual aspect, his falcon eye softened by affection as he looked down on his fair child; she the image of himself, only more graceful and brilliant in expression. I was reminded of Southey's Kehama; when, lo, the dream was rudely broken! They were talking of education, and he said,

" I shall not have Maria brought too forward. If she knows too much, she will never find a husband; superior women hardly ever can."

"Surely," said his wife, with a blush, " you wish Maria to be as good and wise as she can, whether it will help her to marriage or not."

" No," he persisted, " I want her to have a sphere and a home, and some one to protect her when I am gone."

It was a trifling incident, but made a deep impression. I felt that the holiest relations fail to instruct the unprepared and perverted mind. If this man, indeed, could have looked at it on the other side, he was the last that would have been willing to have been taken himself for the home and protection he could give, but would have been much more likely to repeat the tale of Alcibiades with his phials.

But men do *not* look at both sides, and women must leave off asking them and being influenced by them, but retire within themselves, and explore the ground-work of life till they find their peculiar secret. Then, when they come forth again, renovated and baptized, they will know how to turn all dross to gold, and will be rich and free though they live in a hut, tranquil if in a crowd. Then their sweet singing shall not be from passionate impulse, but the lyrical overflow of a divine rapture, and a new music shall be evolved from this many-chorded world.

Grant her, then, for a while, the armor and the javelin. Let her put from her the press of other minds, and meditate in virgin loneliness. The same idea shall reäppear in due time as Muse, or Ceres, the all-kindly, patient Earth-Spirit.

Among the throng of symptoms which denote the present tendency to a crisis in the life of Woman, — which resembles the change from girlhood, with its beautiful instincts, but unharmonized thoughts, its blind pupilage and restless seeking, to self-possessed, wise and graceful womanhood,— I have attempted to select a few.

One of prominent interest is the unison upon the subject of three male minds, which, for width of culture, power of self-concentration and dignity of aim, take rank as the prophets of the coming age, while their histories and labors are rooted in the past.

Swedenborg came, he tells us, to interpret the past revelation and unfold a new. He announces the New Church that is to prepare the way for the New Jerusalem, a city built of precious stones, hardened and purified by secret processes in the veins of earth through the ages.

Swedenborg approximated to that harmony between the scientific. and poetic lives of mind, which we hope from the perfected man. The links that bind together the realms of nature, the mysteries that accompany her births and growths, were unusually plain to him. He seems a man to whom insight was given at a period when the mental frame was sufficiently matured to retain and express its gifts.

His views of Woman are, in the main, satisfactory. In some details we may object to them, as, in all his system, there are still remains of what is arbitrary and seemingly groundless — fancies that show the marks of old habits, and a nature as yet not thoroughly leavened with the spiritual leaven. At least, so it seems to me now. I speak reverently, for I find such reason to venerate Swedenborg, from an imperfect knowledge of his mind, that I feel one more perfect might explain to me much that does not now secure my sympathy.

His idea of Woman is sufficiently large and noble to interpose no obstacle to her progress. His idea of marriage is consequently sufficient. Man and Woman share an angelic ministry; the union is of one with one, permanent and pure.

As the New Church extends its ranks, the needs of Woman must be more considered.

Quakerism also establishes Woman on a sufficient equality with Man. But, though the original thought of Quakerism is pure, its scope is too narrow, and its influence, having established a certain amount of good and made clear some truth, must, by degrees, be merged in one of wider range.* The mind of Swedenborg appeals to the various nature of Man, and allows room for æsthetic culture and the free expression of energy.

As apostle of the new order, of the social fabric that is to rise from love, and supersede the old that was based on strife, Charles Fourier comes next, expressing, in an outward order, many facts of which Swedenborg saw the secret springs. The mind of Fourier, though grand and clear, was, in some respects, superficial. He was a stranger to the highest experiences. His eye was fixed on the outward more than the inward needs of Man. Yet he, too, was a seer of the divine order, in its musical expression, if not in its poetic soul. He has filled one department of instruction for the new era, and the harmony in action, and freedom for individual growth, he hopes, shall exist; and, if the methods he proposes should not prove the true ones, yet his fair propositions shall

---

* In worship at stated periods, in daily expression, whether by word or deed, the Quakers have placed Woman on the same platform with Man. Can any one assert that they have reason to repent this?

give many hints, and make room for the inspiration needed for such.

He, too, places Woman on an entire equality with Man, and wishes to give to one as to the other that independence which must result from intellectual and practical development.

Those who will consult him for no other reason, might do so to see how the energies of Woman may be made available in the pecuniary way. The object of Fourier was to give her the needed means of self-help, that she might dignify and unfold her life for her own happiness, and that of society. The many, now, who see their daughters liable to destitution, or vice to escape from it, may be interested to examine the means, if they have not yet soul enough to appreciate the ends he proposes.

On the opposite side of the advancing army leads the great apostle of individual culture, Goethe. Swedenborg makes organization and union the necessary results of solitary thought. Fourier, whose nature was, above all, constructive, looked to them too exclusively. Better institutions, he thought, will make better men. Goethe expressed, in every way, the other side. If one man could present better forms, the rest could not use them till ripe for them.

Fourier says, As the institutions, so the men! All follies are excusable and natural under bad institutions.

Goethe thinks, As the man, so the institutions! There is no excuse for ignorance and folly. A man can grow in any place, if he will.

Ay! but, Goethe, bad institutions are prison-walls and

impure air, that make him stupid, so that he does not will.

And thou, Fourier, do not expect to change mankind at once, or even "in three generations," by arrangement of groups and series, or flourish of trumpets for attractive industry. If these attempts are made by unready men, they will fail.

Yet we prize the theory of Fourier no less than the profound suggestion of Goethe. Both are educating the age to a clearer consciousness of what Man needs, what Man can be; and better life must ensue.

Goethe, proceeding on his own track, elevating the human being, in the most imperfect states of society, by continual efforts at self-culture, takes as good care of women as of men. His mother, the bold, gay Frau Aja, with such playful freedom of nature; the wise and gentle maiden, known in his youth, over whose sickly solitude " the Holy Ghost brooded as a dove ; " his sister, the intellectual woman *par excellence ;* the Duchess Amelia; Lili, who combined the character of the woman of the world with the lyrical sweetness of the shepherdess, on whose chaste and noble breast flowers and gems were equally at home; all these had supplied abundant suggestions to his mind, as to the wants and the possible excellences of Woman. And from his poetic soul grew up forms new and more admirable than life has yet produced, for whom his clear eye marked out paths in the future.

In Faust Margaret represents the redeeming power, which, at present, upholds Woman, while waiting for a

better day. The lovely little girl, pure in instinct,
ignorant in mind, is misled and profaned by man abusing
her confidence.*   To the Mater *Dolorosa* she appeals for
aid. It is given to the soul, if not against outward sorrow ; and the maiden, enlightened by her sufferings,
refusing to receive temporal salvation by the aid of an
evil power, obtains the eternal in its stead.

In the second part, the intellectual man, after all his
manifold strivings, owes to the interposition of her whom
he had betrayed *his* salvation.   She intercedes, this time,
herself a glorified spirit, with the Mater *Gloriosa.*

Leonora, too, is Woman, as we see her now, pure,
thoughtful, refined by much acquaintance with grief.

Iphigenia he speaks of in his journals as his " daughter," and she is the daughter † whom a man will wish,
even if he has chosen his wife from very mean motives.
She is the virgin, steadfast soul, to whom falsehood is
more dreadful than any other death.

But it is to Wilhelm Meister's Apprenticeship and

* As Faust says, her only fault was a " kindly delusion," — " ein
guter wahn."

† Goethe was as false to his ideas, in practice, as Lord Herbert. And
his punishment was the just and usual one of connections formed beneath the standard of right, from the impulses of the baser self.   Iphigenia was the worthy daughter of his mind ; but the son, child of his
degrading connection in actual life, corresponded with that connection.
This son, on whom Goethe vainly lavished so much thought and care,
was like his mother, and like Goethe's attachment for his mother.
" This young man," says a late well-informed writer (M. Henri
Blaze), " Wieland, with good reason, called the son of the servant, *der
Sohn der Magd.* He inherited from his father only his name and his
physique."

Wandering Years that I would especially refer, as these
volumes contain the sum of the Sage's observations during
a long life, as to what Man should do, under present circumstances, to obtain mastery over outward, through an
initiation into inward life, and severe discipline of faculty.

As Wilhelm advances into the upward path, he becomes
acquainted with better forms of Woman, by knowing how
to seek, and how to prize them when found. For the
weak and immature man will, often, admire a superior
woman, but he will not be able to abide by a feeling
which is too severe a tax on his habitual existence. But,
with Wilhelm, the gradation is natural, and expresses
ascent in the scale of being. At first, he finds charm in
Mariana and Philina, very common forms of feminine
character, not without redeeming traits, no less than
charms, but without wisdom or purity. Soon he is attended by Mignon, the finest expression ever yet given
to what I have called the lyrical element in Woman.
She is a child, but too full-grown for this man ; he loves,
but cannot follow her ; yet is the association not without
an enduring influence. Poesy has been domesticated in
his life ; and, though he strives to bind down her heavenward impulse, as art or apothegm, these are only the
tents, beneath which he may sojourn for a while, but
which may be easily struck, and carried on limitless
wanderings.

Advancing into the region of thought, he encounters
a wise philanthropy in Natalia (instructed, let us observe, by an *uncle*) ; practical judgment and the outward

economy of life in Theresa; pure devotion in the Fair Saint.

Further, and last, he comes to the house of Macaria, the soul of a star; that is, a pure and perfected intelligence embodied in feminine form, and the centre of a world whose members revolve harmoniously around her. She instructs him in the archives of a rich human history, and introduces him to the contemplation of the heavens.

From the hours passed by the side of Mariana to these with Macaria, is a wide distance for human feet to traverse. Nor has Wilhelm travelled so far, seen and suffered so much, in vain. He now begins to study how he may aid the next generation; he sees objects in harmonious arrangement, and from his observations deduces precepts by which to guide his course as a teacher and a master, "help-full, comfort-full."

In all these expressions of Woman, the aim of Goethe is satisfactory to me. He aims at a pure self-subsistence, and a free development of any powers with which they may be gifted by nature as much for them as for men. They are units, addressed as souls. Accordingly, the meeting between Man and Woman, as represented by him, is equal and noble; and, if he does not depict marriage, he makes it possible.

In the Macaria, bound with the heavenly bodies in fixed revolutions, the centre of all relations, herself unrelated, he expresses the Minerva side of feminine nature. It was not by chance that Goethe gave her this name. Macaria, the daughter of Hercules, who offered herself as a victim for the good of her country, was canonized by the Greeks, and worshipped as the Goddess of true Felicity. Goethe has embodied this Felicity as the Serenity that arises from Wisdom, a Wisdom such as the Jewish wise man venerated, alike instructed in the designs of heaven, and the methods necessary to carry them into effect upon earth.

Mignon is the electrical, inspired, lyrical nature. And wherever it appears we echo in our aspirations that of the child,

> "So let me seem until I be : —
> Take not the *white robe* away."
>
> * * * * *
>
> "Though I lived without care and toil,
> Yet felt I sharp pain enough :
> Make me again forever young."

All these women, though we see them in relations, we can think of as unrelated. They all are very individual, yet seem nowhere restrained. They satisfy for the present, yet arouse an infinite expectation.

The economist Theresa, the benevolent Natalia, the fair Saint, have chosen a path, but their thoughts are not narrowed to it. The functions of life to them are not ends, but suggestions.

Thus, to them, all things are important, because none is necessary. Their different characters have fair play, and each is beautiful in its minute indications, for nothing is enforced or conventional ; but everything, however slight, grows from the essential life of the being.

Mignon and Theresa wear male attire when they like, and it is graceful for them to do so, while Macaria is confined to her arm-chair behind the green curtain, and the Fair Saint could not bear a speck of dust on her robe.

All things are in their places in this little world, because all is natural and free, just as "there is room for everything out of doors." Yet all is rounded in by natural harmony, which will always arise where Truth and Love are sought in the light of Freedom.

Goethe's book bodes an era of freedom like its own of "extraordinary, generous seeking," and new revelations. New individualities shall be developed in the actual world, which shall advance upon it as gently as the figures come out upon his canvas.

I have indicated on this point the coincidence between his hopes and those of Fourier, though his are directed by an infinitely higher and deeper knowledge of human nature.   But, for our present purpose, it is sufficient to show how surely these different paths have conducted to the same end two earnest thinkers.   In some other place I wish to point out similar coincidences between Goethe's model school and the plans of Fourier, which may cast light upon the page of prophecy.

Many women have observed that the time drew nigh for a better care of the sex, and have thrown out hints that may be useful.   Among these may be mentioned —

Miss Edgeworth, who, although restrained by the habits of her age and country, and belonging more to the eighteenth than the nineteenth century, has done excellently as far as she goes.   She had a horror of sentimentalism, and of the love of notoriety, and saw how likely

women, in the early stages of culture, were to aim at
these. Therefore she bent her efforts to recommending
domestic life. But the methods she recommends are such
as will fit a character for any position to which it may be
called. She taught a contempt of falsehood, no less in
its most graceful, than in its meanest apparitions; the
cultivation of a clear, independent judgment, and adher-
ence to its dictates; habits of various and liberal study
and employment, and a capacity for friendship. Her
standard of character is the same for both sexes,— Truth,
honor, enlightened benevolence, and aspiration after
knowledge. Of poetry, she knows nothing, and her
religion consists in honor and loyalty to obligations once
assumed — in short, in "the great idea of duty which
holds us upright." Her whole tendency is practical.

Mrs. Jameson is a sentimentalist, and, therefore, suits
us ill, in some respects, but she is full of talent, has a
just and refined perception of the beautiful, and a genuine courage when she finds it necessary. She does not
appear to have thought out, thoroughly, the subject on
which we are engaged, and her opinions, expressed as
opinions, are sometimes inconsistent with one another.
But from the refined perception of character, admirable
suggestions are given in her "Women of Shakspeare,"
and "Loves of the Poets."

But that for which I most respect her is the decision
with which she speaks on a subject which refined women
are usually afraid to approach, for fear of the insult and
scurrile jest they may encounter; but on which she
neither can nor will restrain the indignation of a full

heart. I refer to the degradation of a large portion of women into the sold and polluted slaves of men, and the daring with which the legislator and man of the world lifts his head beneath the heavens, and says, "This must be; it cannot be helped; it is a necessary accompaniment of *civilization*."

So speaks the *citizen*. Man born of Woman, the father of daughters, declares that he will and must buy the comforts and commercial advantages of his London, Vienna, Paris, New York, by conniving at the moral death, the damnation, so far as the action of society can insure it, of thousands of women for each splendid metropolis.

O men! I speak not to you. It is true that your wickedness (for you must not deny that at least nine thousand out of the ten fall through the vanity you have systematically flattered, or the promises you have treacherously broken); yes, it is true that your wickedness is its own punishment. Your forms degraded and your eyes clouded by secret sin; natural harmony broken and fineness of perception destroyed in your mental and bodily organization; God and love shut out from your hearts by the foul visitants you have permitted there; incapable of pure marriage; incapable of pure parentage; incapable of worship; O wretched men, your sin is its own punishment! You have lost the world in losing yourselves. Who ruins another has admitted the worm to the root of his own tree, and the fuller ye fill the cup of evil, the deeper must be your own bitter draught. But I speak not to you — you need to teach and warn one

another.   And more than one voice rises in earnestness.
And all that *women* say to the heart that has once chosen the evil path is considered prudery, or ignorance, or
perhaps a feebleness of nature which exempts from similar temptations.

But to you, women, American women, a few words
may not be addressed in vain.   One here and there may
listen.

You know how it was in the Oriental clime.   One
man, if wealth permitted, had several wives and many
handmaidens.   The chastity and equality of genuine
marriage, with " the thousand decencies that flow " from
its communion, the precious virtues that gradually may
be matured within its enclosure, were unknown.

But this man did not wrong according to his light.
What he did, he might publish to God and Man ; it was
not a wicked secret that hid in vile lurking-places and
dens, like the banquets of beasts of prey.   Those women
were not lost, not polluted in their own eyes, nor those
of others.   If they were not in a state of knowledge and
virtue, they were at least in one of comparative innocence.

You know how it was with the natives of this con-
tinent.   A chief had many wives, whom he maintained
and who did his household work ; those women were but
servants, still they enjoyed the respect of others and
their own.   They lived together in peace.   They knew
that a sin against what was in their nation esteemed
virtue, would be as strictly punished in Man as in Woman.

Now pass to the countries where marriage is between
one and one.   I will not speak of the Pagan nations,

but come to those which own the Christian rule. We all know what that enjoins ; there is a standard to appeal to.

See, now, not the mass of the people, for we all know that it is a proverb and a bitter jest to speak of the " down-trodden million." We know that, down to our own time, a principle never had so fair a chance to pervade the mass of the people, but that we must solicit its illustration from select examples.

Take the Paladin, take the Poet. Did *they* believe purity more impossible to Man than to Woman ? Did they wish Woman to believe that Man was less amenable to higher motives,— that pure aspirations would not guard him against bad passions,— that honorable employments and temperate habits would not keep him free from slavery to the body ? O no ! Love was to them a part of heaven, and they could not even wish to receive its happiness, unless assured of being worthy of it. Its highest happiness to them was that it made them wish to be worthy. They courted probation. They wished not the title of knight till the banner had been upheld in the heats of battle, amid the rout of cowards.

I ask of you, young girls — I do not mean *you* whose heart is that of an old coxcomb, though your locks have not yet lost their sunny tinge. Not of you whose whole character is tainted with vanity, inherited or taught, who have early learned the love of coquettish excitement, and whose eyes rove restlessly in search of a " conquest " or a " beau ;" you who are ashamed *not* to be seen by others the mark of the most contemptuous flattery or injurious desire. To such I do not speak. But to thee, maiden,

who, if not so fair, art yet of that unpolluted nature
which Milton saw when he dreamed of Comus and the
Paradise. Thou, child of an unprofaned wedlock, brought
up amid the teachings of the woods and fields, kept
fancy-free by useful employment and a free flight into
the heaven of thought, loving to please only those whom
thou wouldst not be ashamed to love; I ask of thee,
whose cheek has not forgotten its blush nor thy heart its
lark-like hopes, if he whom thou mayest hope the Father
will send thee, as the companion of life's toils and joys,
is not to thy thought pure? Is not manliness to thy
thought purity, *not* lawlessness? Can his lips speak
falsely? Can he do, in secret, what he could not avow
to the mother that bore him? O say, dost thou not look
for a heart free, open as thine own, all whose thoughts
may be avowed, incapable of wronging the innocent, or
still further degrading the fallen — a man, in short, in
whom brute nature is entirely subject to the impulses of
his better self?

Yes! it was thus that thou didst hope; for I have
many, many times seen the image of a future life, of a
destined spouse, painted on the tablets of a virgin heart.

It might be that she was not true to these hopes. She
was taken into what is called "the world," froth and
scum as it mostly is on the social caldron. There, she
saw fair Woman carried in the waltz close to the heart of
a being who appeared to her a Satyr. Being warned by
a male friend that he was in fact of that class, and not fit
for such familiar nearness to a chaste being, the advised
replied that "women should know nothing about such

things." She saw one fairer given in wedlock to a man
of the same class. " Papa and mamma said that ' all
men were faulty at some time in their lives ; they had
a great many temptations.' Frederick would be so happy
at home; he would not want to do wrong." She turned
to the married women; they, O tenfold horror! laughed
at her supposing " men were like women." Sometimes,
I say, she was not true, and either sadly accommodated
herself to " Woman's lot," or acquired a taste for satyr-
society, like some of the Nymphs, and all the Bacchanals
of old. But to those who could not and would not
accept a mess of pottage, or a Circe cup, in lieu of their
birthright, and to these others who have yet their choice
to make, I say, Courage! I have some words of cheer
for you. A man, himself of unbroken purity, reported
to me the words of a foreign artist, that " the world
would never be better till men subjected themselves to
the same laws they had imposed on women;" that artist,
he added, was true to the thought. The same was true
of Canova, the same of Beethoven. " Like each other
demi-god, they kept themselves free from stain;" and
Michael Angelo, looking over here from the loneliness
of his century, might meet some eyes that need not shun
his glance.

In private life, I am assured by men who are not so
sustained and occupied by the worship of pure beauty,
that a similar consecration is possible, is practised; that
many men feel that no temptation can be too strong for
the will of man, if he invokes the aid of the Spirit
instead of seeking extenuation from the brute alliances

of his nature. In short, what the child fancies is really
true, though almost the whole world declares it a lie.
Man is a child of God; and if he seeks His guidance to
keep the heart with diligence, it will be so given that all
the issues of life may be pure. Life will then be a
temple.

> The temple round
> Spread green the pleasant ground ;
> The fair colonnade
> Be of pure marble pillars made ;
> Strong to sustain the roof,
> Time and tempest proof ;
> Yet, amidst which, the lightest breeze
> Can play as it please ;
> The audience hall
> Be free to all
> Who revere
> The power worshipped here,
> Sole guide of youth,
> Unswerving Truth.
> In the inmost shrine
> Stands the image divine,
> Only seen
> By those whose deeds have worthy been —
> Priestlike clean.
> Those, who initiated are,
> Declare,
> As the hours
> Usher in varying hopes and powers ;
> It changes its face,
> It changes its age,
> Now a young, beaming grace,
> Now Nestorian sage :
> But, to the pure in heart,
> This shape of primal art

> In age is fair,
>   In youth seems wise,
> Beyond compare,
>   Above surprise ;
> What it teaches native seems,
>   Its new lore our ancient dreams ;
> Incense rises from the ground ;
>   Music flows around ;
> Firm rest the feet below, clear gaze the eyes above,
> When Truth, to point the way through life, assumes the wand of Love;
> But, if she cast aside the robe of green,
>   Winter's silver sheen,
>   White, pure as light,
> Makes gentle shroud as worthy weed as bridal robe had been.*

We are now in a transition state, and but few steps have yet been taken. From polygamy, Europe passed to the marriage *de convenance*. This was scarcely an improvement. An attempt was then made to substitute genuine marriage (the mutual choice of souls inducing a permanent union), as yet baffled on every side by the haste, the ignorance, or the impurity of Man.

Where Man assumes a high principle to which he is not yet ripened, it will happen, for a long time, that the few will be nobler than before; the many, worse. Thus now. In the country of Sidney and Milton, the metrop-

---

* As described by the historian : —

" The temple of Juno is like what the character of Woman should be.
Columns ! graceful decorums, attractive yet sheltering.
Porch ! noble, inviting aspect of the life.
Kaos ! receives the worshippers. See here the statue of the Divinity.
Ophistodomos ! Sanctuary where the most precious possessions were kept safe from the hand of the spoiler and the eye of the world."

olis is a den of wickedness, and a sty of sensuality; in the country of Lady Russell, the custom of English peeresses, of selling their daughters to the highest bidder, is made the theme and jest of fashionable novels by unthinking children who would stare at the idea of sending them to a Turkish slave-dealer, though the circumstances of the bargain are there less degrading, as the will and thoughts of the person sold are not so degraded by it, and it is not done in defiance of an acknowledged law of right in the land and the age.

I must here add that I do not believe there ever was put upon record more depravation of Man, and more despicable frivolity of thought and aim in Woman, than in the novels which purport to give the picture of English fashionable life, which are read with such favor in our drawing-rooms, and give the tone to the manners of some circles.   Compared with the cold, hard-hearted folly there described, crime is hopeful; for it, at least, shows some power remaining in the mental constitution.

To return: — Attention has been awakened among men to the stains of celibacy, and the profanations of marriage.   They begin to write about it and lecture about it. It is the tendency now to endeavor to help the erring by showing them the physical law.   This is wise and excellent; but forget not the better half.   Cold bathing and exercise will not suffice to keep a life pure, without an inward baptism, and noble, exhilarating employment for the thoughts and the passions.   Early marriages are desirable, but if (and the world is now so out of joint that there are a hundred thousand chances to one against it) a man does not early, or at all, find the person to whom he can be united in the marriage of souls, will you give him in the marriage *de convenance?* or, if not married, can you find no way for him to lead a virtuous and happy life? Think of it well, ye who think yourselves better than pagans, for many of *them* knew this sure way.*

To you, women of America, it is more especially my business to address myself on this subject, and my advice may be classed under three heads :

Clear your souls from the taint of vanity.

Do not rejoice in conquests, either that your power to allure may be seen by other women, or for the pleasure of rousing passionate feelings that gratify your love of excitement.

GUILT OF
AROUSING
LOVE

It must happen, no doubt, that frank and generous women will excite love they do not reciprocate, but, in nine cases out of ten, the woman has, half consciously, done much to excite. In this case, she shall not be held guiltless, either as to the unhappiness or injury of the lover. Pure love, inspired by a worthy object, must ennoble

* The Persian sacred books, the Desatir, describe the great and holy prince Ky Khosrou, as being " an angel, and the son of an angel," one to whom the Supreme says, " Thou art not absent from before me for one twinkling of an eye. I am never out of thy heart. And I am contained in nothing but in thy heart, and in a heart like thy heart. And I am nearer unto thee than thou art to thyself." This prince had in his Golden Seraglio three ladies of surpassing beauty, and all four, in this royal monastery, passed their lives, and left the world as virgins.

The Persian people had no scepticism when the history of such a mind was narrated.

and bless, whether mutual or not; but that which is excited by coquettish attraction of any grade of refinement, must cause bitterness and doubt, as to the reality of human goodness, so soon as the flush of passion is over. And, that you may avoid all taste for these false pleasures,

> " Steep the soul
> In one pure love, and it will last thee long."

The love of truth, the love of excellence, whether you clothe them in the person of a special object or not, will have power to save you from following Duessa, and lead you in the green glades where Una's feet have trod.

It was on this one subject that a venerable champion of good, the last representative of the spirit which sanctified the Revolution, and gave our country such a sunlight of hope in the eyes of the nations, the same who lately, in Boston, offered anew to the young men the pledge taken by the young men of his day, offered, also, his counsel, on being addressed by the principal of a girl's school, thus : —

REPLY OF MR. ADAMS.

Mr. Adams was so deeply affected by the address of Miss Foster, as to be for some time inaudible. When heard, he spoke as follows :

" This is the first instance in which a lady has thus addressed me personally; and I trust that all the ladies present will be able sufficiently to enter into my feelings to know that I am more affected by this honor than by any other I could have received.

" You have been pleased, madam, to allude to the character of my father, and the history of my family, and their services to the country. It is indeed true that, from the existence of the republic as an independent nation, my father and myself have been in the public service of the country, almost without interruption. I came into the world, as a person having personal responsibilities, with the Declaration of Independence, which constituted us a nation. I was a child at that time, and had then perhaps the greatest of blessings that can be bestowed on man — a mother who was anxious and capable to form her children to be what they ought to be. From that mother I derived whatever instruction — religious especially and moral — has pervaded a long life; I will not say perfectly, and as it ought to be; but I will say, because it is justice only to the memory of her whom I revere, that if, in the course of my life, there has been any imperfection, or deviation from what she taught me, the fault is mine, and not hers.

" With such a mother, and such other relations with the sex, of sister, wife, and daughter, it has been the perpetual instruction of my life to love and revere the female sex. And in order to carry that sentiment of love and reverence to its highest degree of perfection, I know of nothing that exists in human society better adapted to produce that result, than institutions of the character that I have now the honor to address.

" I have been taught, as I have said, through the

course of my life, to love and to revere the female sex; but I have been taught, also — and that lesson has perhaps impressed itself on my mind even more strongly, it may be, than the other — I have been taught not to flatter them. It is not unusual, in the intercourse of Man with the other sex — and especially for young men — to think that the way to win the hearts of ladies is by flattery. To love and to revere the sex, is what I think the duty of Man; but *not to flatter them;* and this I would say to the young ladies here — and if they, and others present, will allow me, with all the authority which nearly four score years may have with those who have not yet attained one score — I would say to them what I have no doubt they say to themselves, and are taught here, not to take the flattery of men as proof of perfection.

"I am now, however, I fear, assuming too much of a character that does not exactly belong to me. I therefore conclude, by assuring you, madam, that your reception of me has affected me, as you perceive, more than I can express in words; and that I shall offer my best prayers, till my latest hour, to the Creator of us all, that this institution especially, and all others of a similar kind, designed to form the female mind to wisdom and virtue, may prosper to the end of time."

It will be interesting to add here the character of Mr. Adams' mother, as drawn by her husband, the first John Adams, in a family letter * written just before his death.

" I have reserved for the last the life of Lady Russell.

* Journal and Correspondence of Miss Adams, vol. I., p. 246.

This I have not yet read, because I read it more than forty years ago. On this hangs a tale which you ought to know and communicate it to your children. I bought the Life and Letters of Lady Russell in the year 1775, and sent it to your grandmother, with an express intent and desire that she should consider it a mirror in which to contemplate herself; for, at that time, I thought it extremely probable, from the daring and dangerous career I was determined to run, that she would one day find herself in the situation of Lady Russell, her husband without a head. This lady was more beautiful than Lady Russell, had a brighter genius, more information, a more refined taste, and, at least, her equal in the virtues of the heart; equal fortitude and firmness of character, equal resignation to the will of Heaven, equal in all the virtues and graces of the Christian life. Like Lady Russell, she never, by word or look, discouraged me from running all hazards for the salvation of my country's liberties; she was willing to share with me, and that her children should share with us both, in all the dangerous consequences we had to hazard."

Will a woman who loves flattery or an aimless excitement, who wastes the flower of her mind on transitory sentiments, ever be loved with a love like that, when fifty years' trial have entitled to the privileges of " the golden marriage ? "

Such was the love of the iron-handed warrior for her, not his hand-maid, but his help-meet :

" Whom God loves, to him gives he such a wife."

I find the whole of what I want in this relation, in the

two epithets by which Milton makes Adam address *his* wife.

In the intercourse of every day he begins :

" Daughter of God and man, *accomplished* Eve." *

In a moment of stronger feeling,

" Daughter of God and man, IMMORTAL Eve."

What majesty in the cadence of the line; what dignity, what reverence in the attitude both of giver and receiver !

The woman who permits, in her life, the alloy of vanity ; the woman who lives upon flattery, coarse or fine, shall never be thus addressed. She is *not* immortal so far as her will is concerned, and every woman who does so creates miasma, whose spread is indefinite. The hand which casts into the waters of life a stone of offence knows not how far the circles thus caused may spread their agitations.

A little while since I was at one of the most fashionable places of public resort. I saw there many women, dressed without regard to the season or the demands of the place, in apery, or, as it looked, in mockery, of European fashions. I saw their eyes restlessly courting attention. I saw the way in which it was paid ; the style of devotion, almost an open sneer, which it pleased those ladies to receive from men whose expression marked their own low position in the moral and intellectual world. Those women went to their pillows with their

* See Appendix H.

heads full of folly, their hearts of jealousy, or gratified vanity; those men, with the low opinion they already entertained of Woman confirmed. These were American *ladies;* that is, they were of that class who have wealth and leisure to make full use of the day, and confer benefits on others. They were of that class whom the possession of external advantages makes of pernicious example to many, if these advantages be misused.

Soon after, I met a circle of women, stamped by society as among the most degraded of their sex. " How," it was asked of them, " did you come here ? " for by the society that I saw in the former place they were shut up in a prison. The causes were not difficult to trace : love of dress, love of flattery, love of excitement. They had not dresses like the other ladies, so they stole them ; they could not pay for flattery by distinctions, and the dower of a worldly marriage, so they paid by the profanation of their persons. In excitement, more and more madly sought from day to day, they drowned the voice of conscience.

Now I ask you, my sisters, if the women at the fashionable house be not answerable for those women being in the prison ?

As to position in the world of souls, we may suppose the women of the prison stood fairest, both because they had misused less light, and because loneliness and sorrow had brought some of them to feel the need of better life, nearer truth and good. This was no merit in them, being an effect of circumstance, but it was hopeful. But you, my friends (and some of you I have already

met), consecrate yourselves without waiting for reproof, in free love and unbroken energy, to win and to
diffuse a better life. Offer beauty, talents, riches, on the
altar ; thus shall ye keep spotless your own hearts, and
be visibly or invisibly the angels to others.

I would urge upon those women who have not yet considered this subject, to do so.   Do not forget the unfor-
tunates who dare not cross your guarded way.   If it do
not suit you to act with those who have organized
measures of reform, then hold not yourself excused from
acting in private.   Seek out these degraded women, give
them tender sympathy, counsel, employment.   Take the
place of mothers, such as might have saved them
originally.

If you can do little for those already under the ban of
the world, — and the best-considered efforts have often
failed, from a want of strength in those unhappy ones to
bear up against the sting of shame and the prejudices of
the world, which makes them seek oblivion again in their
old excitements, — you will at least leave a sense of love
and justice in their hearts, that will prevent their becoming utterly embittered and corrupt.   And you may learn
the means of prevention for those yet uninjured.   These
will be found in a diffusion of mental culture, simple
tastes, best taught by your example, a genuine self-
respect, and, above all, what the influence of Man tends
to hide from Woman, the love and fear of a divine, in
preference to a human tribunal.

But suppose you save many who would have lost their
bodily innocence (for as to mental, the loss of that is

incalculably more general), through mere vanity and
folly ; there still remain many, the prey and spoil of the
brute passions of Man ; for the stories frequent in our
newspapers outshame antiquity, and vie with the horrors
of war.

As to this, it must be considered that, as the vanity
and proneness to seduction of the imprisoned women
represented a general degradation in their sex ; so do
these acts a still more general and worse in the male.
Where so many are weak, it is natural there should be
many lost ; where legislators admit that ten thousand
prostitutes are a fair proportion to one city, and husbands
tell their wives that it is folly to expect chastity from
men, it is inevitable that there should be many monsters
of vice.

I must in this place mention, with respect and gratitude, the conduct of Mrs. Child in the case of Amelia
Norman. The action and speech of this lady was of
straightforward nobleness, undeterred by custom or cavil
from duty toward an injured sister. She showed the case
and the arguments the counsel against the prisoner had the
assurance to use in their true light to the public. She
put the case on the only ground of religion and equity.
She was successful in arresting the attention of many
who had before shrugged their shoulders, and let sin pass
as necessarily a part of the company of men. They
begin to ask whether virtue is not possible, perhaps necessary, to Man as well as to Woman. They begin to
fear that the perdition of a woman must involve that of

LYDIA MARIA
CHILD AND
ARTICLE IN
ADVOCATE
(SEE BERG
p. 210)
HER DEFENSE
OF A ♀ WHO
STABBED A
LICENTIOUS ♂

a man. This is a crisis. The results of this case will be important.

In this connection I must mention Eugene Sue, the French novelist, several of whose works have been lately translated among us, as having the true spirit of reform as to women. Like every other French writer, he is still tainted with the transmissions of the old *regime.* Still, falsehood may be permitted for the sake of advancing truth, evil as the way to good. Even George Sand, who would trample on every graceful decorum, and every human law, for the sake of a sincere life, does not see that she violates it by making her heroines able to tell falsehoods in a good cause. These French writers need ever to be confronted by the clear perception of the English and German mind, that the only good man, consequently the only good reformer, is he

> " Who bases good on good alone, and owes
> To virtue every triumph that he knows."

Still, Sue has the heart of a reformer, and especially towards women; he sees what they need, and what causes are injuring them. From the histories of Fleur de Marie and La Louve, from the lovely and independent character of Rigolette, from the distortion given to Matilda's mind, by the present views of marriage, and from the truly noble and immortal character of the " humpbacked Sempstress " in the " Wandering Jew," may be gathered much that shall elucidate doubt and direct inquiry on this subject. In reform, as in philosophy, the French are the interpreters to the civilized world.

Their own attainments are not great, but they make clear the past, and break down barriers to the future.

Observe that the good man of Sue is as pure as Sir Charles Grandison.

Apropos to Sir Charles. Women are accustomed to be told by men that the reform is to come *from them.* "You," say the men, "must frown upon vice; you must decline the attentions of the corrupt; you must not submit to the will of your husband when it seems to you unworthy, but give the laws in marriage, and redeem it from its present sensual and mental pollutions."

This seems to us hard. Men have, indeed, been, for more than a hundred years, rating women for countenancing vice. But, at the same time, they have carefully hid from them its nature, so that the preference often shown by women for bad men arises rather from a confused idea that they are bold and adventurous, acquainted with regions which women are forbidden to explore, and the curiosity that ensues, than a corrupt heart in the woman. As to marriage, it has been inculcated on women, for centuries, that men have not only stronger passions than they, but of a sort that it would be shameful for them to share or even understand; that, therefore, they must "confide in their husbands," that is, submit implicitly to their will; that the least appearance of coldness or withdrawal, from whatever cause, in the wife is wicked, because liable to turn her husband's thoughts to illicit indulgence; for a man is so constituted that he must indulge his passions or die!

Accordingly, a great part of women look upon men as

a kind of wild beasts, but "suppose they are all alike;" the unmarried are assured by the married that, "if they knew men as they do," that is, by being married to them, "they would not expect continence or self-government from them."

I might accumulate illustrations on this theme, drawn from acquaintance with the histories of women, which would startle and grieve all thinking men, but I forbear. Let Sir Charles Grandison preach to his own sex; or if none there be who feels himself able to speak with authority from a life unspotted in will or deed, let those who are convinced of the practicability and need of a pure life, as the foreign artist was, advise the others, and warn them by their own example, if need be.

The following passage, from a female writer, on female affairs, expresses a prevalent way of thinking on this subject:

"It may be that a young woman, exempt from all motives of vanity, determines to take for a husband a man who does not inspire her with a very decided inclination. Imperious circumstances, the evident interest of her family, or the danger of suffering celibacy, may explain such a resolution. If, however, she were to endeavor to surmount a personal repugnance, we should look upon this as *injudicious.* Such a rebellion of nature marks the limit that the influence of parents, or the self-sacrifice of the young girl, should never pass. *We shall be told that this repugnance is an affair of the imagination.* It may be so; but imagination is a power which it is temerity to brave ; and its antipathy is more difficult to conquer than its preference." *

Among ourselves, the exhibition of such a repugnance from a woman who had been given in marriage " by advice of friends," was treated by an eminent physician as sufficient proof of insanity. If he had said sufficient cause for it, he would have been nearer right.

It has been suggested by men who were pained by seeing bad men admitted, freely, to the society of modest women, — thereby encouraged to vice by impunity, and corrupting the atmosphere of homes,— that there should be a senate of the matrons in each city and town, who should decide what candidates were fit for admission to their houses and the society of their daughters. †

Such a plan might have excellent results ; but it argues a moral dignity and decision which does not yet exist, and needs to be induced by knowledge and reflection.   It has been the tone to keep women ignorant on these subjects, or, when they were not, to command that they should seem so.   "It is indelicate," says the father or husband, " to inquire into the private character of such an one.   It is sufficient that I do not think him unfit to visit you."   And so, this man, who would not tolerate these pages in his house, "unfit for family reading," because they speak plainly, introduces there a man whose shame is written on his brow, as well as the open secret of the whole town, and, presently, if *respectable* still,

* Madame Necker de Saussure.

† See Goethe's Tasso.   "A synod of good women should decide," — if the golden age is to be restored.

and rich enough, gives him his daughter to wife. The mother affects ignorance, "supposing he is no worse than most men." The daughter *is* ignorant; something in the mind of the new spouse seems strange to her, but she supposes it is "woman's lot" not to be perfectly happy in her affections ; she has always heard, "men could not understand women," so she weeps alone, or takes to dress and the duties of the house. The husband, of course, makes no avowal, and dreams of no redemption.

" In the heart of every young woman," says the female writer above quoted, addressing herself to the husband, "depend upon it, there is a fund of exalted ideas; she conceals, represses, without succeeding in smothering them. *So long as these ideas in your wife are directed to* YOU, *they are, no doubt, innocent,* but take care that they be not accompanied with *too much* pain. In other respects, also, spare her delicacy. Let all the antecedent parts of your life, if there are such, which would give her pain, be concealed from her ; *her happiness and her respect for you would suffer from this misplaced confidence.* Allow her to retain that flower of purity, *which should distinguish her, in your eyes, from every other woman.*" We should think so, truly, under this canon. Such a man must esteem purity an exotic that could only be preserved by the greatest care. Of the degree of mental intimacy possible, in such a marriage, let every one judge for himself !

On this subject, let every woman, who has once begun to think, examine herself; see whether she does not suppose virtue possible and necessary to Man, and whether she would not desire for her son a virtue which aimed at a fitness for a divine life, and involved, if not asceticism, that degree of power over the lower self, which shall "not exterminate the passions, but keep them chained at the feet of reason." The passions, like fire, are a bad master; but confine them to the hearth and the altar, and they give life to the social economy, and make each sacrifice meet for heaven.

When many women have thought upon this subject, some will be fit for the senate, and one such senate in operation would affect the morals of the civilized world.

At present I look to the young. As preparatory to the senate, I should like to see a society of novices, such as the world has never yet seen, bound by no oath, wearing no badge. In place of an oath, they should have a religious faith in the capacity of Man for virtue; instead of a badge, should wear in the heart a firm resolve not to stop short of the destiny promised him as a son of God. Their service should be action and conservatism, not of old habits, but of a better nature, enlightened by hopes that daily grow brighter.

If sin was to remain in the world, it should not be by their connivance at its stay, or one moment's concession to its claims.

They should succor the oppressed, and pay to the upright the reverence due in hero-worship by seeking to emulate them. They would not denounce the willingly bad, but they could not be with them, for the two classes could not breathe the same atmosphere.

They would heed no detention from the time-serving, the worldly and the timid.

They could love no pleasures that were not innocent and capable of good fruit.

I saw, in a foreign paper, the title now given to a party abroad, " Los Exaltados." Such would be the title now given these children by the world : Los Exaltados, Las Exaltadas ; but the world would not sneer always, for from them would issue a virtue by which it would, at last, be exalted too.

I have in my eye a youth and a maiden whom I look to as the nucleus of such a class. They are both in early youth ; both as yet uncontaminated ; both aspiring, without rashness ; both thoughtful ; both capable of deep affection ; both of strong nature and sweet feelings ; both capable of large mental development. They reside in different regions of earth, but their place in the soul is the same. To them I look, as, perhaps, the harbingers and leaders of a new era, for never yet have I known minds so truly virgin, without narrowness or ignorance.

When men call upon women to redeem them, they mean such maidens. But such are not easily formed under the present influences of society. As there are more such young men to help give a different tone, there will be more such maidens.

The English, novelist, D'Israeli, has, in his novel of " The Young Duke," made a man of the most depraved stock be redeemed by a woman who despises him when he has only the brilliant mask of fortune and beauty to cover the poverty of his heart and brain, but knows how to encourage him when he enters on a better course. But this woman was educated by a father who valued character in women.

Still, there will come now and then one who will, as I hope of my young Exaltada, be example and instruction for the rest. It was not the opinion of Woman current among Jewish men that formed the character of the mother of Jesus.

Since the sliding and backsliding men of the world, no less than the mystics, declare that, as through Woman Man was lost, so through Woman must Man be redeemed, the time must be at hand. When she knows herself indeed as " accomplished," still more as " immortal Eve," this may be.

As an immortal, she may also know and inspire immortal love, a happiness not to be dreamed of under the circumstances advised in the last quotation. Where love is based on concealment, it must, of course, disappear when the soul enters the scene of clear vision !

And, without this hope, how worthless every plan, every bond, every power !

" The giants," said the Scandinavian Saga, " had induced Loke (the spirit that hovers between good and ill) to steal for them Iduna (Goddess of Immortality) and her apples of pure gold. He lured her out, by promising to show, on a marvellous tree he had discovered, apples beautiful as her own, if she would only take them with her for a comparison. Thus having lured her beyond the heavenly domain, she was seized and carried away captive by the powers of misrule.

"As now the gods could not find their friend Iduna, they were confused with grief; indeed, they began visibly to grow old and gray. Discords arose, and love grew cold. Indeed, Odur, spouse of the goddess of love and beauty, wandered away, and returned no more. At last, however, the gods, discovering the treachery of Loke, obliged him to win back Iduna from the prison in which she sat mourning. He changed himself into a falcon, and brought her back as a swallow, fiercely pursued by the Giant King, in the form of an eagle. So she strives to return among us, light and small as a swallow. We must welcome her form as the speck on the sky that assures the glad blue of Summer. Yet one swallow does not make a summer. Let us solicit them in flights and flocks!"

Returning from the future to the present, let us see what forms Iduna takes, as she moves along the declivity of centuries to the valley where the lily flower may concentrate all its fragrance.

It would seem as if this time were not very near to one fresh from books, such as I have of late been — no: *not* reading, but sighing over. A crowd of books having been sent me since my friends knew me to be engaged in this way, on Woman's "Sphere," Woman's "Mission," and Woman's "Destiny," I believe that almost all that is extant of formal precept has come under my eye. Among these I read with refreshment a little one called "The Whole Duty of Woman," "indited by a noble lady at the request of a noble lord," and which has

this much of nobleness, that the view it takes is a religious one. It aims to fit Woman for heaven ; the main bent
of most of the others is to fit her to please, or, at least,
not to disturb, a husband.

Among these I select, as a favorable specimen, the
book I have already quoted, " The Study* of the Life
of Woman, by Madame Necker de Saussure, of Geneva,
translated from the French."   This book was published
at Philadelphia, and has been read with much favor here.
Madame Necker is the cousin of Madame de Stael, and
has taken from her works the motto prefixed to this.

" Cette vie n'a quelque prix que si elle sert a' l'education morale de notre cœur."

Mde. Necker is, by nature, capable of entire consist-
ency in the application of this motto, and, therefore, the
qualifications she makes, in the instructions given to her
own sex, show forcibly the weight which still paralyzes
and distorts the energies of that sex.

The book is rich in passages marked by feeling and
good suggestions ; but, taken in the whole, the impression
it leaves is this :

Woman is, and *shall remain*, inferior to Man and
subject to his will, and, in endeavoring to aid her, we
must anxiously avoid anything that can be misconstrued
into expression of the contrary opinion, else the men will
be alarmed, and combine to defeat our efforts.

The present is a good time for these efforts, for men
are less occupied about women than formerly.   Let us,

* This title seems to be incorrectly translated from the French. I
have not seen the original.

then, seize upon the occasion, and do what we can to make our lot tolerable. But we must sedulously avoid encroaching on the territory of Man. If we study natural history, our observations may be made useful, by some male naturalist; if we draw well, we may make our services acceptable to the artists. But our names must not be known; and, to bring these labors to any result, we must take some man for our head, and be his hands.

The lot of Woman is sad. She is constituted to expect and need a happiness that cannot exist on earth. She must stifle such aspirations within her secret heart, and fit herself, as well as she can, for a life of resignations and consolations.

She will be very lonely while living with her husband. She must not expect to open her heart to him fully, or that, after marriage, he will be capable of the refined service of love. The man is not born for the woman, only the woman for the man. " Men cannot understand the hearts of women." The life of Woman must be outwardly a well-intentioned, cheerful dissimulation of her real life.

Naturally, the feelings of the mother, at the birth of a female child, resemble those of the Paraguay woman, described by Southey as lamenting in such heart-breaking tones that her mother did not kill her the hour she was born, — " her mother, who knew what the life of a woman must be ; " — or of those women seen at the north by Sir A. Mackenzie, who performed this pious duty towards female infants whenever they had an opportunity.

" After the first delight, the young mother experiences

feelings a little different, according as the birth of a son or a daughter has been announced.

" Is it a son? A sort of glory swells at this thought the heart of the mother; she seems to feel that she is entitled to gratitude. She has given a citizen, a defender, to her country; to her husband an heir of his name; to herself a protector. And yet the contrast of all these fine titles with this being, so humble, soon strikes her. At the aspect of this frail treasure, opposite feelings agitate her heart; she seems to recognize in him *a nature superior to her own*, but subjected to a low condition, and she honors a future greatness in the object of extreme compassion. Somewhat of that respect and adoration for a feeble child, of which some fine pictures offer the expression in the features of the happy Mary, seem reproduced with the young mother who has given birth to a son.

" Is it a daughter? There is usually a slight degree of regret; so deeply rooted is the idea of the superiority of Man in happiness and dignity; and yet, as she looks upon this child, she is more and more *softened* towards it. A deep sympathy — a sentiment of identity with this delicate being — takes possession of her; an extreme pity for so much weakness, a more pressing need of prayer, stirs her heart. Whatever sorrows she may have felt, she dreads for her daughter; but she will guide her to become much wiser, much better than herself. And then the gayety, the frivolity of the young woman have their turn. This little creature is a flower to cultivate, a doll to decorate."

Similar sadness at the birth of a daughter I have heard mothers express not unfrequently.

As to this living so entirely for men, I should think when it was proposed to women they would feel, at least, some spark of the old spirit of races allied to our own. "If he is to be my bridegroom *and lord*," cries Brunhilda,* "he must first be able to pass through fire and water." "I will serve at the banquet," says the Walkyrie, "but only him who, in the trial of deadly combat, has shown himself a hero."

If women are to be bond-maids, let it be to men superior to women in fortitude, in aspiration, in moral power, in refined sense of beauty! You who give yourselves "to be supported," or because "one must love something," are they who make the lot of the sex such that mothers are sad when daughters are born.

It marks the state of feeling on this subject that it was mentioned, as a bitter censure on a woman who had influence over those younger than herself, — "She makes those girls want to see heroes?"

"And will that hurt them?"

"Certainly; how *can* you ask? They will find none, and so they will never be married."

"*Get* married" is the usual phrase, and the one that correctly indicates the thought; but the speakers, on this occasion, were persons too outwardly refined to use it. They were ashamed of the word, but not of the thing. Madame Necker, however, sees good possible in celibacy.

Indeed, I know not how the subject could be better

---

* See the Nibelungen Lays.

illustrated, than by separating the wheat from the chaff in Madame Necker's book; place them in two heaps, and then summon the reader to choose; giving him first a near-sighted glass to examine the two;—it might be a Christian, an astronomical, or an artistic glass,— any kind of good glass to obviate acquired defects in the eye. I would lay any wager on the result.

But time permits not here a prolonged analysis.   I have given the clues for fault-finding.

As a specimen of the good take the following passage, on the phenomena of what I have spoken of, as the lyrical or electric element in Woman.

"Women have been seen to show themselves poets in the most pathetic pantomimic scenes, where all the passions were depicted full of beauty ; and these poets used a language unknown to themselves, and, the performance once over, their inspiration was a forgotten dream. Without doubt there is an interior development to beings so gifted; but their sole mode of communication with us is their talent.   They are, in all besides, the inhabitants of another planet."

Similar observations have been made by those who have seen the women at Irish wakes, or the funeral ceremonies of modern Greece or Brittany, at times when excitement gave the impulse to genius; but, apparently, without a thought that these rare powers belonged to no other planet, but were a high development of the growth of this, and might, by wise and reverent treatment, be made to inform and embellish the scenes of every day. But, when Woman has her fair chance, she will do so, and the poem of the hour will vie with that of the ages.

I come now with satisfaction to my own country, and to a writer, a female writer, whom I have selected as the clearest, wisest, and kindliest, who has, as yet, used pen here on these subjects.   This is Miss Sedgwick.

Miss Sedgwick, though she inclines to the private path, and wishes that, by the cultivation of character, might should vindicate right, sets limits nowhere, and her objects and inducements are pure.   They are the free and careful cultivation of the powers that have been given, with an aim at moral and intellectual perfection. Her speech is moderate and sane, but never palsied by fear or sceptical caution.

Herself a fine example of the independent and benefi- cent existence that intellect and character can give to Woman, no less than Man, if she know how to seek and prize it,—also, that the intellect need not absorb or weak- en, but rather will refine and invigorate, the affections,— the teachings of her practical good sense come with great force, and cannot fail to avail much.   Every way her writings please me both as to the means and the ends.   I am pleased at the stress she lays on observance of the physical laws, because the true reason is given.   Only in a strong and clean body can the soul do its message fitly.

She shows the meaning of the respect paid to personal neatness, both in the indispensable form of cleanliness, and of that love of order and arrangement, that must issue from a true harmony of feeling.

The praises of cold water seem to me an excellent

sign in the age. They denote a tendency to the true life. We are now to have, as a remedy for ills, not orvietan, or opium, or any quack medicine, but plenty of air and water, with due attention to warmth and freedom in dress, and simplicity of diet.

Every day we observe signs that the natural feelings on these subjects are about to be reïnstated, and the body to claim care as the abode and organ of the soul ; not as the tool of servile labor, or the object of voluptuous indulgence.

A poor woman, who had passed through the lowest grades of ignominy, seemed to think she had never been wholly lost, " for," said she, " I would always have good under-clothes ; " and, indeed, who could doubt that this denoted the remains of private self-respect in the mind ?

A woman of excellent sense said, " It might seem childish, but to her one of the most favorable signs of the times was that the ladies had been persuaded to give up corsets."

Yes ! let us give up all artificial means of distortion. Let life be healthy, pure, all of a piece. Miss Sedgwick, in teaching that domestics must have the means of bathing as much as their mistresses, and time, too, to bathe, has symbolized one of the most important of human rights.

Another interesting sign of the time is the influence exercised by two women, Miss Martineau and Miss Barrett, from their sick-rooms. The lamp of life which, if it had been fed only by the affections, depended on precarious human relations, would scarce have been able to maintain a feeble glare in the lonely prison, now shines far and wide over the nations, cheering fellow-sufferers and hallowing the joy of the healthful.

These persons need not health or youth, or the charms of personal presence, to make their thoughts available. A few more such, and " old woman " * shall not be the synonyme for imbecility, nor " old maid " a term of contempt, nor Woman be spoken of as a reed shaken by the wind.

It is time, indeed, that men and women both should cease to grow old in any other way than as the tree does, full of grace and honor. The hair of the artist turns white, but his eye shines clearer than ever, and we feel that age brings him maturity, not decay. So would it be with all, were the springs of immortal refreshment but unsealed within the soul; then, like these women, they would see, from the lonely chamber window, the glories of the universe; or, shut in darkness, be visited by angels.

I now touch on my own place and day, and, as I write, events are occurring that threaten the fair fabric approached by so long an avenue. Week before last, the Gentile was requested to aid the Jew to return to Palestine; for the Millennium, the reign of the Son of Mary was near. Just now, at high and solemn mass, thanks were returned to the Virgin for having delivered O'Connell from unjust imprisonment, in requital of his having consecrated to her the league formed in behalf of Liberty

---

* An apposite passage is quoted in Appendix F.

on Tara's Hill. But last week brought news which threatens that a cause identical with the enfranchisement of Jews, Irish, women, ay, and of Americans in general, too, is in danger, for the choice of the people threatens to rivet the chains of slavery and the leprosy of sin permanently on this nation, through the Annexation of Texas!

Ah! if this should take place, who will dare again to feel the throb of heavenly hope, as to the destiny of this country? The noble thought that gave unity to all our knowledge, harmony to all our designs, — the thought that the progress of history had brought on the era, the tissue of prophecies pointed out the spot, where humanity was, at last, to have a fair chance to know itself, and all men be born free and equal for the eagle's flight, — flutters as if about to leave the breast, which, deprived of it, will have no more a nation, no more a home on earth.

Women of my country! — Exaltadas! if such there be, — women of English, old English nobleness, who understand the courage of Boadicea, the sacrifice of Godiva, the power of Queen Emma to tread the red-hot iron unharmed, — women who share the nature of Mrs. Hutchinson, Lady Russell, and the mothers of our own revolution, — have you nothing to do with this? You see the men, how they are willing to sell shamelessly the happiness of countless generations of fellow-creatures, the honor of their country, and their immortal souls, for a money market and political power. Do you not feel within you that which can reprove them, which can check, which can convince them? You would not speak in vain; whether each in her own home, or banded in unison.

Tell these men that you will not accept the glittering baubles, spacious dwellings, and plentiful service, they mean to offer you through these means. Tell them that the heart of Woman demands nobleness and honor in Man, and that, if they have not purity, have not mercy, they are no longer fathers, lovers, husbands, sons of yours.

This cause is your own, for, as I have before said, there is a reason why the foes of African Slavery seek more freedom for women; but put it not upon that ground, but on the ground of right.

If you have a power, it is a moral power. The films of interest are not so close around you as around the men. If you will but think, you cannot fail to wish to save the country from this disgrace. Let not slip the occasion, but do something to lift off the curse incurred by Eve.

You have heard the women engaged in the Abolition movement accused of boldness, because they lifted the voice in public, and lifted the latch of the stranger. But were these acts, whether performed judiciously or no, *so* bold as to dare before God and Man to partake the fruits of such offence as this?

You hear much of the modesty of your sex. Preserve it by filling the mind with noble desires that shall ward off the corruptions of vanity and idleness. A profligate woman, who left her accustomed haunts and took service in a New York boarding-house, said "she had never heard talk so vile at the Five Points, as from the ladies at the boarding-house." And why? Because they were idle; because, having nothing worthy to engage them, they dwelt, with unnatural curiosity, on the ill they dared not go to see.

It will not so much injure your modesty to have your name, by the unthinking, coupled with idle blame, as to have upon your soul the weight of not trying to save a whole race of women from the scorn that is put upon *their* modesty.

Think of this well! I entreat, I conjure you, before it is too late. It is my belief that something effectual might be done by women, if they would only consider the subject, and enter upon it in the true spirit,— a spirit gentle, but firm, and which feared the offence of none, save One who is of purer eyes than to behold iniquity.

And now I have designated in outline, if not in fulness, the stream which is ever flowing from the heights of my thought.

In the earlier tract I was told I did not make my meaning sufficiently clear. In this I have consequently tried to illustrate it in various ways, and may have been guilty of much repetition. Yet, as I am anxious to leave no room for doubt, I shall venture to retrace, once more, the scope of my design in points, as was done in old-fashioned sermons.

Man is a being of two-fold relations, to nature beneath, and intelligences above him. The earth is his school, if not his birth-place; God his object; life and thought his means of interpreting nature, and aspiring to God.

Only a fraction of this purpose is accomplished in the life of any one man. Its entire accomplishment is to be hoped only from the sum of the lives of men, or Man considered as a whole.

As this whole has one soul and one body, any injury or obstruction to a part, or to the meanest member, affects the whole. Man can never be perfectly happy or virtuous, till all men are so.

To address Man wisely, you must not forget that his life is partly animal, subject to the same laws with Nature.

But you cannot address him wisely unless you consider him still more as soul, and appreciate the conditions and destiny of soul.

The growth of Man is two-fold, masculine and feminine.

So far as these two methods can be distinguished, they are so as

Energy and Harmony ;

Power and Beauty ;

Intellect and Love ;

or by some such rude classification ; for we have not language primitive and pure enough to express such ideas with precision.

These two sides are supposed to be expressed in Man and Woman, that is, as the more and the less, for the faculties have not been given pure to either, but only in preponderance. There are also exceptions in great number, such as men of far more beauty than power, and the reverse. But, as a general rule, it seems to have been the intention to give a preponderance on the one side, that is called masculine, and on the other, one that is called feminine.

There cannot be a doubt that, if these two developments were in perfect harmony, they would correspond to and fulfil one another, like hemispheres, or the tenor and bass in music.

But there is no perfect harmony in human nature; and the two parts answer one another only now and then; or, if there be a persistent consonance, it can only be traced at long intervals, instead of discoursing an obvious melody.

What is the cause of this?

Man, in the order of time, was developed first; as energy comes before harmony; power before beauty.

Woman was therefore under his care as an elder. He might have been her guardian and teacher.

HEGEL

But, as human nature goes not straight forward, but by excessive action and then reäction in an undulated course, he misunderstood and abused his advantages, and became her temporal master instead of her spiritual sire.

On himself came the punishment. He educated Woman more as a servant than a daughter, and found himself a king without a queen.

The children of this unequal union showed unequal natures, and, more and more, men seemed sons of the handmaid, rather than princess.

At last, there were so many Ishmaelites that the rest

grew frightened and indignant. They laid the blame on Hagar, and drove her forth into the wilderness.

But there were none the fewer Ishmaelites for that.

At last men became a little wiser, and saw that the infant Moses was, in every case, saved by the pure instincts of Woman's breast. For, as too much adversity is better for the moral nature than too much prosperity, Woman, in this respect, dwindled less than Man, though in other respects still a child in leading-strings.

So Man did her more and more justice, and grew more and more kind.

But yet — his habits and his will corrupted by the past — he did not clearly see that Woman was half himself; that her interests were identical with his; and that, by the law of their common being, he could never reach his true proportions while she remained in any wise shorn of hers.

And so it has gone on to our day; both ideas developing, but more slowly than they would under a clearer recognition of truth and justice, which would have permitted the sexes their due influence on one another, and mutual improvement from more dignified relations.

Wherever there was pure love, the natural influences were, for the time, restored.

Wherever the poet or artist gave free course to his genius, he saw the truth, and expressed it in worthy forms, for these men especially share and need the feminine principle. The divine birds need to be brooded into life and song by mothers.

Wherever religion (I mean the thirst for truth and

good, not the love of sect and dogma) had its course, the original design was apprehended in its simplicity, and the dove presaged sweetly from Dodona's oak.

I have aimed to show that no age was left entirely without a witness of the equality of the sexes in function, duty and hope.

Also that, when there was unwillingness or ignorance, which prevented this being acted upon, women had not the less power for their want of light and noble freedom. But it was power which hurt alike them and those against whom they made use of the arms of the servile, — cunning, blandishment, and unreasonable emotion.

That now the time has come when a clearer vision and better action are possible — when Man and Woman may regard one another as brother and sister, the pillars of one porch, the priests of one worship.

I have believed and intimated that this hope would receive an ampler fruition, than ever before, in our own land.

And it will do so if this land carry out the principles from which sprang our national life.

I believe that, at present, women are the best helpers of one another.

Let them think; let them act; till they know what they need.

We only ask of men to remove arbitrary barriers. Some would like to do more. But I believe it needs that Woman show herself in her native dignity, to teach them how to aid her; their minds are so encumbered by tradition.

When Lord Edward Fitzgerald travelled with the Indians, his manly heart obliged him at once to take the packs from the squaws and carry them. But we do not read that the red men followed his example, though they are ready enough to carry the pack of the white woman, because she seems to them a superior being.

Let Woman appear in the mild majesty of Ceres, and rudest churls will be willing to learn from her.

You ask, what use will she make of liberty, when she has so long been sustained and restrained?

I answer; in the first place, this will not be suddenly given. I read yesterday a debate of this year on the subject of enlarging women's rights over property. It was a leaf from the class-book that is preparing for the needed instruction. The men learned visibly as they spoke. The champions of Woman saw the fallacy of arguments on the opposite side, and were startled by their own convictions. With their wives at home, and the readers of the paper, it was the same. And so the stream flows on; thought urging action, and action leading to the evolution of still better thought.

But, were this freedom to come suddenly, I have no fear of the consequences. Individuals might commit excesses, but there is not only in the sex a reverence for decorums and limits inherited and enhanced from generation to generation, which many years of other life could not efface, but a native love, in Woman as Woman, of proportion, of "the simple art of not too much,"— a Greek moderation, which would create immediately a restraining party, the natural legislators and instructors of the rest, and would gradually establish such rules as are needed to guard, without impeding, life.

The Graces would lead the choral dance, and teach the rest to regulate their steps to the measure of beauty.

But if you ask me what offices they may fill, I reply — any. I do not care what case you put; let them be sea-captains, if you will. I do not doubt there are women well fitted for such an office, and, if so, I should be as glad to see them in it, as to welcome the maid of Saragossa, or the maid of Missolonghi, or the Suliote heroine, or Emily Plater.

I think women need, especially at this juncture, a much greater range of occupation than they have, to rouse their latent powers. A party of travellers lately visited a lonely hut on a mountain. There they found an old woman, who told them she and her husband had lived there forty years. "Why," they said, "did you choose so barren a spot?" She "did not know; *it was the man's notion.*"

And, during forty years, she had been content to act, without knowing why, upon "the man's notion." I would not have it so.

In families that I know, some little girls like to saw wood, others to use carpenters' tools. Where these tastes are indulged, cheerfulness and good-humor are promoted. Where they are forbidden, because "such things are not proper for girls," they grow sullen and mischievous.

Fourier had observed these wants of women, as no one can fail to do who watches the desires of little girls, or knows the ennui that haunts grown women, except where

they make to themselves a serene little world by art of
some kind. He, therefore, in proposing a great variety
of employments, in manufactures or the care of plants
and animals, allows for one third of women as likely to
have a taste for masculine pursuits, one third of men for
feminine.

Who does not observe the immediate glow and serenity
that is diffused over the life of women, before restless or
fretful, by engaging in gardening, building, or the lowest
department of art? Here is something that is not routine,
something that draws forth life towards the infinite.

I have no doubt, however, that a large proportion of
women would give themselves to the same employments
as now, because there are circumstances that must lead
them. Mothers will delight to make the nest soft and
warm. Nature would take care of that; no need to clip
the wings of any bird that wants to soar and sing, or finds
in itself the strength of pinion for a migratory flight
unusual to its kind. The difference would be that *all*
need not be constrained to employments for which *some*
are unfit.

I have urged upon the sex self-subsistence in its two
forms of self-reliance and self-impulse, because I believe
them to be the needed means of the present juncture.

I have urged on Woman independence of Man, not
that I do not think the sexes mutually needed by one
another, but because in Woman this fact has led to an
excessive devotion, which has cooled love, degraded marriage, and prevented either sex from being what it should
be to itself or the other.

I wish Woman to live, *first* for God's sake. Then she will not make an imperfect man her god, and thus sink to idolatry. Then she will not take what is not fit for her from a sense of weakness and poverty. Then, if she finds what she needs in Man embodied, she will know how to love, and be worthy of being loved.

By being more a soul, she will not be less Woman, for nature is perfected through spirit.

Now there is no woman, only an overgrown child.

That her hand may be given with dignity, she must be able to stand alone. I wish to see men and women capable of such relations as are depicted by Landor in his Pericles and Aspasia, where grace is the natural garb of strength, and the affections are calm, because deep. The softness is that of a firm tissue, as when

> " The gods approve
> The depth, but not the tumult of the soul,
> A fervent, not ungovernable love."

A profound thinker has said, " No married woman can represent the female world, for she belongs to her husband. The idea of Woman must be represented by a virgin."

But that is the very fault of marriage, and of the present relation between the sexes, that the woman *does* belong to the man, instead of forming a whole with him. Were it otherwise, there would be no such limitation to the thought.

Woman, self-centred, would never be absorbed by any relation; it would be only an experience to her as to

man. It is a vulgar error that love, *a* love, to Woman
is her whole existence; she also is born for Truth and
Love in their universal energy. Would she but assume
her inheritance, Mary would not be the only virgin
mother. Not Manzoni alone would celebrate in his wife
the virgin mind with the maternal wisdom and conjugal
affections. The soul is ever young, ever virgin.

And will not she soon appear?—the woman who shall
vindicate their birthright for all women; who shall
teach them what to claim, and how to use what they
obtain? Shall not her name be for her era Victoria, for
her country and life Virginia? Yet predictions are
rash; she herself must teach us to give her the fitting
name.

An idea not unknown to ancient times has of late been
revived, that, in the metamorphoses of life, the soul
assumes the form, first of Man, then of Woman, and
takes the chances, and reaps the benefits of either lot.
Why then, say some, lay such emphasis on the rights or
needs of Woman? What she wins not as Woman will
come to her as Man.

That makes no difference. It is not Woman, but the
law of right, the law of growth, that speaks in us, and
demands the perfection of each being in its kind — apple
as apple, Woman as Woman. Without adopting your
theory, I know that I, a daughter, live through the life
of Man; but what concerns me now is, that my life be a
beautiful, powerful, in a word, a complete life in its
kind. Had I but one more moment to live I must wish
the same.

Suppose, at the end of your cycle, your great world-year, all will be completed, whether I exert myself or not (and the supposition is *false*, — but suppose it true), am I to be indifferent about it? Not so! I must beat my own pulse true in the heart of the world; for *that* is virtue, excellence, health.

Thou, Lord of Day! didst leave us to-night so calmly glorious, not dismayed that cold winter is coming, not postponing thy beneficence to the fruitful summer! Thou didst smile on thy day's work when it was done, and adorn thy down-going as thy up-rising, for thou art loyal, and it is thy nature to give life, if thou canst, and shine at all events!

I stand in the sunny noon of life. Objects no longer glitter in the dews of morning, neither are yet softened by the shadows of evening. Every spot is seen, every chasm revealed. Climbing the dusty hill, some fair effigies that once stood for symbols of human destiny have been broken; those I still have with me show defects in this broad light. Yet enough is left, even by experience, to point distinctly to the glories of that destiny; faint, but not to be mistaken streaks of the future day. I can say with the bard,

" Though many have suffered shipwreck, still beat noble hearts."

Always the soul says to us all, Cherish your best hopes as a faith, and abide by them in action. Such shall be the effectual fervent means to their fulfilment;

For the Power to whom we bow
Has given its pledge that, if not now,

They of pure and steadfast mind,
By faith exalted, truth refined,
Shall hear all music loud and clear,
Whose first notes they ventured here.
Then fear not thou to wind the horn,
Though elf and gnome thy courage scorn;
Ask for the castle's King and Queen;
Though rabble rout may rush between,
Beat thee senseless to the ground,
In the dark beset thee round;
Persist to ask, and it will come;
Seek not for rest in humbler home;
So shalt thou see, what few have seen,
The palace home of King and Queen.

15th November, 1844.

APPENDIX.

A.

APPARITION of the goddess Isis to her votary, from Apuleius.

" Scarcely had I closed my eyes, when, behold (I saw in a dream), a divine form emerging from the middle of the sea, and raising a countenance venerable even to the gods themselves. Afterward, the whole of the most splendid image seemed to stand before me, having gradually shaken off the sea. I will endeavor to explain to you its admirable form, if the poverty of human language will but afford me the power of an appropriate narration ; or if the divinity itself, of the most luminous form, will supply me with a liberal abundance of fluent diction. In the first place, then, her most copious and long hairs, being gradually intorted, and promiscuously scattered on her divine neck, were softly defluous. A multiform crown, consisting of various flowers, bound the sublime summit of her head. And in the middle of the crown, just on her forehead, there was a smooth orb, resembling a mirror, or rather a white refulgent light, which indicated that she was the moon. Vipers, rising up after the manner of furrows, environed the crown on the right hand and on the left, and Cerealian ears of corn were also extended from above. Her garment was of many colors, and woven from the finest flax, and was at one time lucid with a white splendor, at another yellow, from the flower of crocus, and at another flaming with a rosy redness. But that which most excessively dazzled my sight, was a very black robe, fulgid with a dark splendor, and which, spreading round and passing under her right side, and ascending to her left shoulder, there rose protuberant, like the centre of a shield, the dependent part of her robe falling in many folds, and having small knots of fringe, gracefully flowing in its extremities. Glittering stars were dispersed through the embroidered border of the robe, and through the whole of its surface, and the full moon, shining in the middle of the stars, breathed forth flaming fires. A crown, wholly consisting of flowers and fruits of every kind, adhered with indivisible connection to the border of conspicuous robe, in all its undulating motions.

" What she carried in her hands also consisted of things of a very different nature. Her right hand bore a brazen rattle, through the narrow lamina of which, bent like a belt, certain rods passing, produced a sharp triple sound through the vibrating motion of her arm. An oblong vessel, in the shape of a boat, depended from her left hand, on the handle of which, in that part which was conspicuous, an asp raised its erect head and largely swelling neck. And shoes, woven from the leaves of the victorious palm-tree, covered her immortal feet. Such, and so great a goddess, breathing the fragrant odor of the shores of Arabia the happy, deigned thus to address me."

The foreign English of the translator, Thomas Taylor, gives this description the air of being itself a part of the mysteries. But its majestic beauty requires no formal initiation to be enjoyed.

B.

I GIVE this in the original, as it does not bear translation. Those who read Italian will judge whether it is not a perfect description of a perfect woman.

LODI E PREGHIERE A MARIA.

Vergine bella che di sol vestita,
Coronata di stelle, al sommo Sole
  Piacesti si, che'n te sua luce ascose ;
Amor mi spinge a dir di te parole :
  Ma non so 'ncominciar senza tu' aita,
E di Colui che amando in te si pose.

Invoco lei che ben sempre rispose,
Chi la chiamò con fede.
Vergine, s'a mercede
Miseria extrema dell' smane cose
 Giammai tivolse, al mio prego t'inchina :
Soccorri alla mia guerra ;
 Bench' i' sia terra, e tu del ciel Regina.

Vergine saggia, e del bel numero una
Delle beate vergini prudenti ;
 Anzi la prima, e con più chiara lampa ;
O saldo scudo dell' afflitte gente
 Contra colpi di Morte e di Fortuna,
Sotto' l qual si trionfa, non pur scampa :
 O refrigerio alcieco ardor ch' avvampa
Qui fra mortali sciocchi,
 Vergine, que' begli occhi
Che vider tristi la spietata stampa
 Ne' dolci membri del tuo caro figlio,
Volgi al mio dubbio stato ;
 Che sconsigliato a te vien per consiglio.

Vergine pura, d'ogni parte intera,
Del tuo parto gentil figliuola e madre ;
 Che allumi questa vita, e l'altra adorni ;
Per te il tuo Figlio e quel del sommo Padre,
 O finestra del ciel lucente altera,
Venne a salvarne in su gli estremi giorni,
 E fra tutt' i terreni altri soggiorni
Sola tu fusti eletta,
 Vergine benedetta ;
Che 'l pianto d' Eva in allegrezza torni' ;
 Fammi ; che puoi ; della sua grazia degno,
Senza fine o beata,
 Già coronata nel superno regno.

Vergine santa d'ogni grazia piena ;
Che per vera e altissima umiltate
 Salisti al ciel, onde miei preghi ascolti ;
Tu partoristi il fonte di pietate,
 E di giustizia il Sol, che rasserena

Il secol pien d'errori oscuri e folti :
    Tre dolci e cari nomi ha' in te raccolti,
Madre, Figliuola, e Sposa ;
    Vergine gloriosa,
Donna del Re che nostri lacci ha sciolti,
    E fatto 'l mondo libero e felice ;
Nelle cui sante piaghe
    Prego ch'appaghe il cor, vera beatrice.

    Vergine sola al mondo senza esempio,
Che 'l ciel di tue bellezze innamorasti,
    Cui nè prima fu simil, nè seconda ;
Santi pensieri, atti pietosi e casti
    Al vero Dio sacrato, e vivo tempio
Fecero in tua virginita feconda.
    Per te può la mia vita esser gioconda ;
S' a' tuoi preghi, o MARIA
    Vergine dolce, e pia,
Ove 'l fallo abbondò, la grazia abbonda.
    Con le ginocchia della mente inchine
Prego che sia mia scorta ;
    E la mia torta via drizzi a buon fine.

    Vergine chiara, e stabile in eterno,
Di questo tempestoso mare stella ;
    D'ogni fedel nocchier fidata gui da ;
Pon mente in che terribile procella
    I mi ritrovo sol senza governo,
Ed ho gia' da vicin l'ulti me strida :
    Ma pur' in te l'anima mia si fida ;
Peccatrice ; i' nol nego,
    Vergine : ma te prego
Che 'l tuo nemico del mia mal non rida :
    Ricorditi che fece il peccar nostro
Prender Dio, per scamparne,
    Umana carne al tuo virginal christro.

    Vergine, quante lagrime ho già sparte,
Quante lusinghe, e quanti preghi indarno,
    Pur per mia pena, e per mio grave danno !
Da poi ch' i nacqui in su la riva d'Arno ;

Cercando or questa ed or quell altra parte,
Non è stata mia vita altro ch' affanno.
  Mortal bellezza, atti, e parole m' hanno
Tutta ingombrata l'alma.
  Vergine sacra, ed alma,
Non tardar ; ch' i' non forse all' ultim 'ann,
  I di miei piu correnti che saetta,
Fra miserie e peccati
    Sonsen andati, e sol Morte n'aspetta.

  Vergine, tale è terra, e posto ha in doglia
Lo mio cor ; che vivendo in pianto il tenne ;
  E di mille miei mali un non sapea ;
E per saperlo, pur quel che n'avvenne,
  Fora avvenuto : ch' ogni altra sua voglia
Era a me morte, ed a lei fama rea
  Or tu, donna del ciel, tu nostra Dea,
Se dir lice, e conviensi ;
  Vergine d'alti sensi,
Tu vedi il tutto ; e quel che non potea
  Far altri, è nulla a e la tua gran virtute ;
Pon fine al mio dolore ;
    Ch'a te onore ed a me fia salute.

  Vergine, in cui ho tutta mia speranza
Che possi e vogli al gran bisogno aitarme ;
  Non mi lasciare in su l'estremo passo :
Non guardar me, ma chi degnò crearme ;
  No'l mio valor, ma l'alta sua sembianza ;
Che in me ti mova a curar d'uorm si basso.
  Medusa, e l'error mio io han fatto un sasso
D'umor vano stillante ;
  Vergine, tu di sante
Lagrime, e pie adempi 'l mio cor lasso ;
  Ch' almen l'ultimo pianto sia divoto,
    Senza terrestro limo ;
  Come fu'l primo non d'insania voto.

  Vergine umana, e nemica d'orgoglio,
Del comune principio amor t'induca ;
  Miserere d'un cor contrito umile ;
Che se poca mortal terra caduca

Amar con si mirabil fede soglio ;
Che devro far di te cosa gentile ?
   Se dal mio stato assai misero, e vile
Per le tue man resurgo,
   Vergine ; è' sacro, e purgo
Al tuo nome e pens ieri e'ngegno, e stile ;
   La lingua, e'l cor, le lagrime, e i sospiri,
Scorgimi al miglior guado ;
   E prendi in grado i cangiati desiri.

   Il di s'appressa, e non pote esser lunge ;
Si corre il tempo, e vola,
   Vergine unica, e sola ;
E'l cor' or conscienza, or morte punge.
Raccommandami al tuo Figliuol, verace
   Uomo, e verace Dio ;
   Ch accolga l mio spirto ultimo in pace.

As the Scandinavian represented Frigga the Earth, or World-mother, knowing all things, yet never herself revealing them, though ready to be called to counsel by the gods, it represents her in action, decked with jewels and gorgeously attended. But, says the Mythos, when she ascended the throne of Odin, her consort (Haaven), she left with mortals her friend, the Goddess of Sympathy, to protect them in her absence.

Since, Sympathy goes about to do good. Especially she devotes herself to the most valiant and the most oppressed. She consoles the gods in some degree even for the death of their darling Baldur. Among the heavenly powers she has no consort.

C.

THE WEDDING OF THE LADY THERESA.

FROM LOCKHART'S SPANISH BALLADS.

'T was when the fifth Alphonso in Leon held his sway,
   King Abdalla of Toledo an embassy did send ;
He asked his sister for a wife, and in an evil day
   Alphonso sent her, for he feared Abdalla to offend ;

He feared to move his anger, for many times before
He had received in danger much succor from the Moor.

Sad heart had fair Theresa, when she their paction knew ;
    With streaming tears she heard them tell she 'mong the Moors
        must go ;
That she, a Christian damsel, a Christian firm and true,
    Must wed a Moorish husband, it well might cause her woe ;
But all her tears and all her prayers they are of small avail ;
    At length she for her fate prepares, a victim sad and pale.

The king hath sent his sister to fair Toledo town,
    Where then the Moor Abdalla his royal state did keep ;
When she drew near, the Moslem from his golden throne came down,
    And courteously received her, and bade her cease to weep ;
With loving words he pressed her to come his bower within ;
With kisses he caressed her, but still she feared the sin.

" Sir King, Sir King, I pray thee," — 't was thus Theresa spake, —
    " I pray thee, have compassion, and do to me no wrong ;
For sleep with thee I may not, unless the vows I break,
    Whereby I to the holy church of Christ my Lord belong ;
For thou hast sworn to serve Mahoun, and if this thing should be,
The curse of God it must bring down upon thy realm and thee.

" The angel of Christ Jesu, to whom my heavenly Lord
    Hath given my soul in keeping, is ever by my side ;
If thou dost me dishonor, he will unsheathe his sword,
    And smite thy body fiercely, at the crying of thy bride ;
Invisible he standeth ; his sword like fiery flame
Will penetrate thy bosom the hour that sees my shame."

The Moslem heard her with a smile ; the earnest words she said
    He took for bashful maiden's wile, and drew her to his bower :
In vain Theresa prayed and strove,— she pressed Abdalla's bed,
    Perforce received his kiss of love, and lost her maiden flower.
A woeful woman there she lay, a loving lord beside,
And earnestly to God did pray her succor to provide.

The angel of Christ Jesu her sore complaint did hear,
    And plucked his heavenly weapon from out his sheath unseen :
He waved the brand in his right hand, and to the King came near,
    And drew the point o'er limb and joint, beside the weeping Queen :

A mortal weakness from the stroke upon the King did fall ;
He could not stand when daylight broke, but on his knees must crawl.

Abdalla shuddered inly, when he this sickness felt,
　　And called upon his barons, his pillow to come nigh ;
" Rise up," he said, " my liegemen," as round his bed they knelt,
　　" And take this Christian lady, else certainly I die ;
Let gold be in your girdles, and precious stones beside,
And swiftly ride to Leon, and render up my bride."

When they were come to Leon Theresa would not go
　　Into her brother's dwelling, where her maiden years were spent ;
But o'er her downcast visage a white veil she did throw,
　　And to the ancient nunnery of Las Huelgas went.
There, long, from worldly eyes retired, a holy life she led ;
There she, an aged saint, expired ; there sleeps she with the dead.

D.

THE following extract from Spinoza is worthy of attention, as
expressing the view which a man of the largest intellectual scope
may take of Woman, if that part of his life to which her influence appeals has been left unawakened. He was a man of the
largest intellect, of unsurpassed reasoning powers ; yet he makes
a statement false to history, for we well know how often men and
women have ruled together without difficulty, and one in which
very few men even at the present day — I mean men who are
thinkers, like him — would acquiesce.

I have put in contrast with it three expressions of the latest
literature.

First, from the poems of W. E. Channing, a poem called
" Reverence," equally remarkable for the deep wisdom of its
thought and the beauty of its utterance, and containing as fine a
description of one class of women as exists in literature.

In contrast with this picture of Woman, the happy Goddess of
Beauty, the wife, the friend, " the summer queen," I add one
by the author of " Festus," of a woman of the muse, the sybil
kind, which seems painted from living experience.

And, thirdly, I subjoin Eugene Sue's description of a wicked but able woman of the practical sort, and appeal to all readers whether a species that admits of three such varieties is so easily to be classed away, or kept within prescribed limits, as Spinoza, and those who think like him, believe.

SPINOZA. TRACTATUS POLITICI DE DEMOCRATIA.
CAPUT XI.

Perhaps some one will here ask, whether the supremacy of Man over Woman is attributable to nature or custom? Since, if it be human institutions alone to which this fact is owing, there is no reason why we should exclude women from a share in government. Experience most plainly teaches that it is Woman's weakness which places her under the authority of Man. It has nowhere happened that men and women ruled together ; but wherever men and women are found, the world over, there we see the men ruling and the women ruled, and in this order of things men and women live together in peace and harmony. The Amazons, it is true, are reputed formerly to have held the reins of government, but they drove men from their dominions ; the male of their offspring they invariably destroyed, permitting their daughters alone to live. Now, if women were by nature upon an equality with men, if they equalled men in fortitude, in genius (qualities which give to men might, and consequently right), it surely would be the case, that, among the numerous and diverse nations of the earth, some would be found where both sexes ruled conjointly, and others where the men were ruled by the women, and so educated as to be mentally inferior ; and since this state of things nowhere exists, it is perfectly fair to infer that the rights of women are not equal to those of men ; but that women must be subordinate, and therefore cannot have an equal, far less a superior place in the government. If, too, we consider the passions of men — how the love men feel towards women is seldom anything but lust and impulse, and much less a reverence for qualities of soul than an admiration of physical beauty ; observing, too, the jealousy of lovers, and other things of the same character — we shall see at a glance that it would be, in the high-

est degree, detrimental to peace and harmony, for men and women
to possess an equal share in government.

REVERENCE.

As an ancestral heritage revere
All learning, and all thought.   The painter's fame
Is thine, whate'er thy lot, who honorest grace.
And need enough in this low time, when they,
Who seek to captivate the fleeting notes
Of heaven's sweet beauty, must despair almost,
So heavy and obdurate show the hearts
Of their companions.   Honor kindly then
Those who bear up in their so generous arms
The beautiful ideas of matchless forms ;
For were these not portrayed, our human fate, —
Which is to be all high, majestical,
To grow to goodness with each coming age,
Till virtue leap and sing for joy to see
So noble, virtuous men, — would brief decay ;
And the green, festering slime, oblivious, haunt
About our common fate.   O, honor them !

But what to all true eyes has chiefest charm,
And what to every breast where beats a heart
Framed to one beautiful emotion, — to
One sweet and natural feeling, lends a grace
To all the tedious walks of common life,
This is fair Woman, — Woman, whose applause
Each poet sings, — Woman the beautiful.
Not that her fairest brow, or gentlest form,
Charm us to tears ; not that the smoothest cheek,
Wherever rosy tints have made their home,
So rivet us on her ; but that she is
The subtle, delicate grace, — the inward grace,
For words too excellent ; the noble, true,
The majesty of earth ; the summer queen ;
In whose conceptions nothing but what 's great
Has any right.   And, O ! her love for him,
Who does but his small part in honoring her ;
Discharging a sweet office, sweeter none,

Mother and child, friend, counsel and repose ;
Naught matches with her, naught has leave with her
To highest human praise.   Farewell to him
Who reverences not with an excess
Of faith the beauteous sex ; all barren he
Shall live a living death of mockery.
Ah ! had but words the power, what could we say
Of Woman !   We, rude men of violent phrase,
Harsh action, even in repose inwardly harsh ;
Whose lives walk blustering on high stilts, removed
From all the purely gracious influence
Of mother earth.   To single from the host
Of angel forms one only, and to her
Devote our deepest heart and deepest mind,
Seems almost contradiction.   Unto her
We owe our greatest blessings, hours of cheer,
Gay smiles, and sudden tears, and more than these
A sure perpetual love.   Regard her as
She walks along the vast still earth ; and see !
Before her flies a laughing troop of joys,
And by her side treads old experience,
With never-failing voice admonitory ;
The gentle, though infallible, kind advice,
The watchful care, the fine regardfulness,
Whatever mates with what we hope to find,
All consummate in her — the summer queen.

To call past ages better than what now
Man is enacting on life's crowded stage,
Cannot improve our worth ; and for the world
Blue is the sky as ever, and the stars
Kindle their crystal flames at soft fallen eve
With the same purest lustre that the east
Worshipped.   The river gently flows through fields
Where the broad-leaved corn spreads out, and loads
Its ear as when the Indian tilled the soil.
The dark green pine, — green in the winter's cold, —
Still whispers meaning emblems, as of old ;
The cricket chirps, and the sweet eager birds
In the sad woods crowd their thick melodies ;
But yet, to common eyes, life's poetry

Something has faded, and the cause of this
May be that Man, no longer at the shrine
Of Woman, kneeling with true reverence,
In spite of field, wood, river, stars and sea,
Goes most disconsolate. A babble now,
A huge and wind-swelled babble, fills the place
Of that great adoration which of old
Man had for Woman. In these days no more
Is love the pith and marrow of Man's fate.
Thou who in early years feelest awake
To finest impulses from nature's breath,
And in thy walk hearest such sounds of truth
As on the common ear strike without heed,
Beware of men around thee ! Men are foul
With avarice, ambition and deceit ;
The worst of all, ambition. This is life,
Spent in a feverish chase for selfish ends,
Which has no virtue to redeem its toil,
But one long, stagnant hope to raise the self.
The miser's life to this seems sweet and fair ;
Better to pile the glittering coin, than seek
To overtop our brothers and our loves.
Merit in this ? Where lies it, though thy name
Ring over distant lands, meeting the wind
Even on the extremest verge of the wide world ?
Merit in this ? Better be hurled abroad
On the vast whirling tide, than, in thyself
Concentred, feed upon thy own applause.
Thee shall the good man yield no reverence ;
But, while the idle, dissolute crowd are loud
In voice to send thee flattery, shall rejoice
That he has 'scaped thy fatal doom, and known
How humble faith in the good soul of things
Provides amplest enjoyment. O, my brother
If the Past's counsel any honor claim
From thee, go read the history of those
Who a like path have trod, and see a fate
Wretched with fears, changing like leaves at noon,
When the new wind sings in the white birch wood.
Learn from the simple child the rule of life,
And from the movements of the unconscious tribes

Of animal nature, those that bend the wing
Or cleave the azure tide, content to be,
What the great frame provides, — freedom and grace.
Thee, simple child, do the swift winds obey,
And the white waterfalls with their bold leaps
Follow thy movements.   Tenderly the light
Thee watches, girding with a zone of radiance,
And all the swinging herbs love thy soft steps.

DESCRIPTION OF ANGELA, FROM "FESTUS."

I LOVED her for that she was beautiful,
And that to me she seemed to be all nature
And all varieties of things in one ;
Would set at night in clouds of tears, and rise
All light and laughter in the morning ; fear
No petty customs nor appearances,
But think what others only dreamed about ;
And say what others did but think ; and do
What others would but say ; and glory in
What others dared but do ; it was these which won me ;
And that she never schooled within her breast
One thought or feeling, but gave holiday
To all ; that she told me all her woes,
And wrongs, and ills ; and so she made them mine
In the communion of love ; and we
Grew like each other, for we loved each other ;
She, mild and generous as the sun in spring ;
And I, like earth, all budding out with love.
*   *   *   *   *   *
The beautiful are never desolate ;
For some one alway loves them ; God or man ;
If man abandons, God himself takes them ;
And thus it was.   She whom I once loved died ;
The lightning loathes its cloud ; the soul its clay.
Can I forget the hand I took in mine,
Pale as pale violets ; that eye, where mind
And matter met alike divine ? — ah, no !
May God that moment judge me when I do !
   O ! she was fair ; her nature once all spring
And deadly beauty, like a maiden sword,

Startlingly beautiful.   I see her now !
Wherever thou art thy soul is in my mind ;
Thy shadow hourly lengthens o'er my brain
And peoples all its pictures with thyself ;
Gone, not forgotten ; passed, not lost ; thou wilt shine
In heaven like a bright spot in the sun !
She said she wished to die, and so she died,
For, cloudlike, she poured out her love, which was
Her life, to freshen this parched heart.   It was thus ;
I said we were to part, but she said nothing ;
There was no discord ; it was music ceased,
Life's thrilling, bursting, bounding joy.   She sate,
Like a house-god, her hands fixed on her knee,
And her dark hair lay loose and long behind her,
Through which her wild bright eye flashed like a flint ;
She spake not, moved not, but she looked the more,
As if her eye were action, speech, and feeling.
I felt it all, and came and knelt beside her,
The electric touch solved both our souls together ;
Then came the feeling which unmakes, undoes ;
Which tears the sea-like soul up by the roots,
And lashes it in scorn against the skies.

       *   *   *   *   *

It is the saddest and the sorest sight,
One's own love weeping.   But why call on God ?
But that the feeling of the boundless bounds
All feeling ; as the welkin does the world ;
It is this which ones us with the whole and God.
Then first we wept ; then closed and clung together ;
And my heart shook this building of my breast
Like a live engine booming up and down :
She fell upon me like a snow-wreath thawing.
Never were bliss and beauty, love and woe,
Ravelled and twined together into madness,
As in that one wild hour to which all else
The past is but a picture.   That alone
Is real, and forever there in front.

    *   *   *   *   *

    *   *   * After that I left her,
And only saw her once again alive.

" Mother Saint Perpetua, the superior of the convent, was a tall woman, of about forty years, dressed in dark gray serge, with a long rosary hanging at her girdle. A white mob-cap, with a long black veil, surrounded her thin, wan face with its narrow, hooded border. A great number of deep, transverse wrinkles ploughed her brow, which resembled yellowish ivory in color and substance. Her keen and prominent nose was curved like the hooked beak of a bird of prey ; her black eye was piercing and sagacious ; her face was at once intelligent, firm, and cold.

" For comprehending and managing the material interests of the society, Mother Saint Perpetua could have vied with the shrewdest and most wily lawyer. When women are possessed of what is called *business talent*, and when they apply thereto the sharpness of perception, the indefatigable perseverance, the prudent dissimulation, and, above all, the correctness and rapidity of judgment at first sight, which are peculiar to them, they arrive at prodigious results.

" To Mother Saint Perpetua, a woman of a strong and solid head, the vast moneyed business of the society was but child's play. None better than she understood how to buy depreciated properties, to raise them to their original value, and sell them to advantage; the average purchase of rents, the fluctuations of exchange, and the current prices of shares in all the leading speculations, were perfectly familiar to her. Never had she directed her agents to make a single false speculation, when it had been the question how to invest funds, with which good souls were constantly endowing the society of Saint Mary. She had established in the house a degree of order, of discipline, and, above all, of economy, that were indeed remarkable ; the constant aim of all her exertions being, not to enrich herself, but the community over which she presided ; for the spirit of association, when it is directed to an object of *collective selfishness,* gives to corporations all the faults and vices of individuals."

E.

THE following is an extract from a letter addressed to me by one of the monks of the nineteenth century. A part I have omitted, because it does not express my own view, unless with qualifications which I could not make, except by full discussion of the subject.

" Woman in the Nineteenth Century should be a pure, chaste, holy being.

" This state of being in Woman is no more attained by the expansion of her intellectual capacity, than by the augmentation of her physical force.

" Neither is it attained by the increase or refinement of her love for Man, or for any object whatever, or for all objects collectively ; but

" This state of being is attained by the reference of all her powers and all her actions to the source of Universal Love, whose constant requisition is a pure, chaste and holy life.

" So long as Woman looks to Man (or to society) for that which she needs, she will remain in an indigent state, for he himself is indigent of it, and as much needs it as she does.

" So long as this indigence continues, all unions or relations constructed between Man and Woman are constructed in indigence, and can produce only indigent results or unhappy consequences.

" The unions now constructing, as well as those in which the parties constructing them were generated, being based on self-delight, or lust, can lead to no more happiness in the twentieth than is found in the nineteenth century.

" It is not amended institutions, it is not improved education, it is not another selection of individuals for union, that can meliorate the sad result, but the *basis* of the union must be changed.

" If in the natural order Woman and Man would adhere strictly to physiological or natural laws, in physical chastity, a most beautiful amendment of the human race, and human condition, would in a few generations adorn the world.

" Still, it belongs to Woman in the spiritual order, to devote herself wholly to her eternal husband, and become the Free Bride of the One who alone can elevate her to her true position, and reconstruct her a pure, chaste, and holy being."

F.

I HAVE mislaid an extract from " The Memoirs of an American Lady," which I wished to use on this subject, but its import is, briefly, this :

Observing of how little consequence the Indian women are in youth, and how much in age, because in that trying life, good counsel and sagacity are more prized than charms, Mrs. Grant expresses a wish that reformers would take a hint from observation of this circumstance.

In another place she says : " The misfortune of our sex is, that young women are not regarded as the material from which old women must be made."

I quote from memory, but believe the weight of the remark is retained.

G.

EURIPIDES. SOPHOCLES.

As many allusions are made in the foregoing pages to characters of women drawn by the Greek dramatists, which may not be familiar to the majority of readers, I have borrowed from the papers of Miranda some notes upon them. I trust the girlish toné of apostrophizing rapture may be excused. Miranda was very young at the time of writing, compared with her present mental age. *Now*, she would express the same feelings, but in a worthier garb — if she expressed them at all.

Iphigenia ! Antigone ! you were worthy to live ! *We* are fallen on evil times, my sisters ; our feelings have been checked ; our thoughts questioned ; our forms dwarfed and defaced by a bad nurture. Yet hearts like yours are in our breasts, living, if unawakened ; and our minds are capable of the same resolves. You we understand at once ; those who stare upon us pertly in the street, we cannot — could never understand.

You knew heroes, maidens, and your fathers were kings of men. You believed in your country and the gods of your country. A great occasion was given to each, whereby to test her character.

You did not love on earth ; for the poets wished to show us the force of Woman's nature, virgin and unbiased. You were women ; not wives, or lovers, or mothers. Those are great names, but we are glad to see *you* in untouched flower.

Were brothers so dear, then, Antigone? We have no brothers. We see no men into whose lives we dare look steadfastly, or to whose destinies we look forward confidently. We care not for their urns ; what inscription could we put upon them? They live for petty successes, or to win daily the bread of the day. No spark of kingly fire flashes from their eyes.

None ! are there *none?*

It is a base speech to say it. Yes ! there are some such ; we have sometimes caught their glances. But rarely have they been rocked in the same cradle as we, and they do not look upon us much ; for the time is not yet come.

Thou art so grand and simple! we need not follow thee ; thou dost not need our love.

But, sweetest Iphigenia ! who knew *thee*, as to me thou art known ? I was not born in vain, if only for the heavenly tears I have shed with thee. She will be grateful for them. I have understood her wholly, as a friend should ; better than she understood herself.

With what artless art the narrative rises to the crisis ! The conflicts in Agamemnon's mind, and the imputations of Menelaus, give us, at once, the full image of him, strong in will and pride, weak in virtue, weak in the noble powers of the mind that depend on imagination. He suffers, yet it requires the presence of his daughter to make him feel the full horror of what he is to do.

> " Ah me ! that breast, those cheeks, those golden tresses ! "

It is her beauty, not her misery, that makes the pathos. This is noble. And then, too, the injustice of the gods, that she, this creature of unblemished loveliness, must perish for the sake of a worthless woman. Even Menelaus feels it the moment he recovers from his wrath.

> " What hath she to do,
> The virgin daughter, with my Helena !
>   *   *   Its former reasonings now
> My soul foregoes.   *   *   *   *

> For it is not just
> That thou shouldst groan, while my affairs go pleasantly,
> That those of thy house should die, and mine see the light."

Indeed, the overwhelmed aspect of the king of men might well move him.

> " *Men.* Brother, give me to take thy right hand.
> *Aga.* I give it, *for* the victory is thine, and I am wretched.
> I am, indeed, ashamed to drop the tear,
> And not to drop the tear I am ashamed."

How beautifully is Iphigenia introduced; beaming more and more softly on us with every touch of description! After Clytemnestra has given Orestes (then an infant) out of the chariot, she says:

> " Ye females, in your arms
> Receive her, for she is of tender age.
> Sit here by my feet, my child,
> By thy mother, Iphigenia, and show
> These strangers how I am blessed in thee,
> And here address thee to thy father.
> *Iphi.* O, mother ! should I run, wouldst thou be angry ?
> And embrace my father heart to heart ? "

With the same sweet, timid trust she prefers the request to himself, and, as he holds her in his arms, he seems as noble as Guido's Archangel ; as if he never could sink below the trust of such a being !

The Achilles, in the first scene, is fine. A true Greek hero ; not too good ; all flushed with the pride of youth, but capable of godlike impulses. At first, he thinks only of his own wounded pride (when he finds Iphigenia has been decoyed to Aulis under the pretext of becoming his wife) ; but the grief of the queen soon makes him superior to his arrogant chafings. How well he says,

> "*Far as a young man may*, I will repress
> So great a wrong ! "

By seeing him here, we understand why he, not Hector, was the hero of the Iliad. The beautiful moral nature of Hector was early developed by close domestic ties, and the cause of his country. Except in a purer simplicity of speech and manner, he might be a modern and a Christian. But Achilles is cast in the largest and most vigorous mould of the earlier day. His nature is one of the richest capabilities, and therefore less quickly unfolds its meaning. The impression it makes at the early period is only of power and pride ; running as fleetly with his armor on as with it off ; but sparks of pure lustre are struck, at moments, from the mass of ore. Of this sort is his refusal to see the beautiful virgin he has promised to protect. None of the Grecians must have the right to doubt his motives. How wise and prudent, too, the advice he gives as to the queen's conduct ! He will not show himself unless needed. His pride is the farthest possible remote from vanity. His thoughts are as free as any in our own time.

> " The prophet ? what is he ? a man
> Who speaks, 'mong many falsehoods, but few truths,
> Whene'er chance leads him to speak true ; when false,
> The prophet is no more."

Had Agamemnon possessed like clearness of sight, the virgin would not have perished, but Greece would have had no religion and no national existence.

When, in the interview with Agamemnon, the queen begins her speech, in the true matrimonial style, dignified though her gesture be, and true all she says, we feel that truth, thus sauced with taunts, will not touch his heart, nor turn him from his purpose. But when Iphigenia begins her exquisite speech, as with the breathings of a lute,—

> " Had I, my father, the persuasive voice
> Of Orpheus, &c.
>
> Compel me not
> What is beneath to view. I was the first
> To call thee father ; me thou first didst call
> Thy child. I was the first that on thy knees
> Fondly caressed thee, and from thee received
> The fond caress. This was thy speech to me : —
> ' Shall I, my child, e'er see thee in some house
> Of splendor, happy in thy husband, live
> And flourish, as becomes my dignity ? '

> My speech to thee was, leaning 'gainst thy cheek,
> (Which with my hand I now caress) : ' And what
> Shall I then do for thee ? Shall I receive
> My father when grown old, and in my house
> Cheer him with each fond office, to repay
> The careful nurture which he gave my youth ? '
> These words are in my memory deep impressed ;
> Thou hast forgot them, and will kill thy child."

Then she adjures him by all the sacred ties, and dwells pathetically on the circumstance which had struck even Menelaus.

> " If Paris be enamored of his bride,
> His Helen,— what concerns it me ? and how
> Comes he to my destruction ?
> > Look upon me ;
> Give me a smile, give me a kiss, my father ;
> That, if my words persuade thee not, in death
> I may have this memorial of thy love."

Never have the names of father and daughter been uttered with a holier tenderness than by Euripides, as in this most lovely passage, or in the " Suppliants," after the voluntary death of Evadne. Iphis says :

> " What shall this wretch now do ? Should I return
> To my own house ? — sad desolation there
> I shall behold, to sink my soul with grief.
> Or go I to the house of Capaneus?
> That was delightful to me, when I found
> My daughter there ; but she is there no more.
> Oft would she kiss my cheek, with fond caress
> Oft soothe me. To a father, waxing old,
> Nothing is dearer than a daughter ! Sons
> Have spirits of higher pitch, but less inclined
> To sweet, endearing fondness. Lead me then,
> Instantly lead me to my house ; consign
> My wretched age to darkness, there to pine
> And waste away.
> > Old age,
> Struggling with many griefs, O, how I hate thee !"

But to return to Iphigenia,— how infinitely melting is her appeal to Orestes, whom she holds in her robe!

> " My brother, small assistance canst thou give
> Thy friends ; yet for thy sister with thy tears
> Implore thy father that she may not die.
> Even infants have a sense of ills ; and see,
> My father ! silent though he be, he sues
> To thee. Be gentle to me ; on my life
> Have pity. Thy two children by this beard
> Entreat thee, thy dear children ; one is yet
> An infant, one to riper years arrived."

The mention of Orestes, then an infant, though slight, is of a domestic charm that prepares the mind to feel the tragedy of his after lot. When the queen says,

> " Dost thou sleep,
> My son ? The rolling chariot hath subdued thee ;
> Wake to thy sister's marriage happily,"

we understand the horror of the doom which makes this cherished child a parricide. And so, when Iphigenia takes leave of him after her fate is by herself accepted,—

" *Iphi.* To manhood train Orestes.
Cly. Embrace him, for thou ne'er shalt see him more.
Iphi. (*To Orestes.*) Far as thou couldst, thou didst assist thy friends,"—

we know not how to blame the guilt of the maddened wife and mother. In her last meeting with Agamemnon, as in her previous expostulations and anguish, we see that a straw may turn the balance, and make her his deadliest foe. Just then, came the suit of Ægisthus,— then, when every feeling was uprooted or lacerated in her heart.

Iphigenia's moving address has no further effect than to make her father turn at bay and brave this terrible crisis. He goes out, firm in resolve ; and she and her mother abandon themselves to a natural grief.

Hitherto nothing has been seen in Iphigenia, except the young girl, weak, delicate, full of feeling, and beautiful as a sunbeam on the full, green tree. But, in the next scene, the first impulse of that passion which makes and unmakes us, though unconfessed even to herself, though hopeless and unreturned, raises her at once into the heroic woman, worthy of the goddess who demands her.

Achilles appears to defend her, whom all others clamorously seek to deliver to the murderous knife. She sees him, and, fired with thoughts unknown before, devotes herself at once for the country which has given birth to such a man.

> " To be too fond of life
> Becomes not me ; nor for myself alone,
> But to all Greece, a blessing didst thou bear me.
> Shall thousands, when their country 's injured, lift
> Their shields ? shall thousands grasp the oar and dare,
> Advancing bravely 'gainst the foe, to die
> For Greece ? And shall my life, my single life,
> Obstruct all this ? Would this be just ? What word
> Can we reply ? Nay more, it is not right
> That he with all the Grecians should contest
> In fight, should die, *and for a woman.* No !
> More than a thousand women is one man
> Worthy to see the light of day.
> *   *   *   for Greece I give my life.
> Slay me ! demolish Troy ! for these shall be
> Long time my monuments, my children these,
> My nuptials and my glory."

This sentiment marks Woman, when she loves enough to feel what a creature of glory and beauty a true *Man* would be, as much in our own time as that of Euripides. Cooper makes the weak Hetty say to her beautiful sister :

" Of course, I don't compare you with Harry. A handsome man is always far handsomer than any woman." True, it was the sentiment of the age, but it was the first time Iphigenia had felt it. In Agamemnon she saw *her father ;* to him she could prefer her claim. In Achilles she saw *a Man*, the crown of creation, enough to fill the world with his presence, were all other beings blotted from its spaces.*

The reply of Achilles is as noble.   Here is his bride ; he feels it now, and all his vain vauntings are hushed.

> " Daughter of Agamemnon, highly blest
>   Some god would make me, if I might attain
>   Thy nuptials.   Greece in thee I happy deem,
>   And thee in Greece.   *   *   .
>   *   *   *   in thy thought
>   Revolve this well ; death is a dreadful thing."

How sweet is her reply, — and then the tender modesty with which she addresses him here and elsewhere as " *stranger*."

> " Reflecting not on any, thus I speak :
>   Enough of wars and slaughters from the charms
>   Of Helen rise ; but die not thou for me,
>   O Stranger, nor distain thy sword with blood,
>   But let me save my country if I may.
> *Achilles.*   O glorious spirit ! naught have I 'gainst this
>   To urge, since such thy will, for what thou sayst
>   Is generous.   Why should not the truth be spoken ? "

But feeling that human weakness may conquer yet, he goes to wait at the altar, resolved to keep his promise of protection thoroughly.

In the next beautiful scene she shows that a few tears might overwhelm her in his absence. She raises her mother beyond weeping them, yet her soft purity she cannot impart.

> " *Iphi.* My father, and my husband do not hate :
>   *Cly.* For thy dear sake fierce contests must he bear.
>   *Iphi.* For Greece reluctant me to death he yields ;
>   *Cly.* Basely, with guile unworthy Atreus' son."

* Men do not often reciprocate this pure love.

> " Her prentice han' she tried on man,
>   And then she made the lasses o',"

is a fancy, not a feeling, in their more frequently passionate and strong than noble or tender natures.

This is truth incapable of an answer, and Iphigenia attempts none.

She begins the hymn which is to sustain her :

> " Lead me ; mine the glorious fate,
> To o'erturn the Phrygian state."

After the sublime flow of lyric heroism, she suddenly sinks back into the tenderer feeling of her dreadful fate.

> " O my country, where these eyes
> Opened on Pelasgic skies !
> O ye virgins, once my pride,
> In Mycenæ who abide !
>
> CHORUS.
> Why of Perseus, name the town,
> Which Cyclopean ramparts crown?
>
> IPHIGENIA.
> Me you reared a beam of light,
> Freely now I sink in night."

Freely ; as the messenger afterwards recounts it.

> * * * * * *
>
> " Imperial Agamemnon, when he saw
> His daughter, as a victim to the grave,
> Advancing, groaned, and, bursting into tears,
> Turned from the sight his head, before his eyes,
> Holding his robe. The virgin near him stood,
> And thus addressed him : ' Father, I to thee
> Am present ; for my country, and for all
> The land of Greece, I freely give myself
> A victim : to the altar let them lead me,
> Since such the oracle. If aught on me
> Depends, be happy, and obtain the prize
> Of glorious conquest, and revisit safe
> Your country. Of the Grecians, for this cause,
> Let no one touch me ; with intrepid spirit
> Silent will I present my neck.' She spoke,
> And all that heard revered the noble soul
> And virtue of the virgin."

How quickly had the fair bud bloomed up into its perfection ! Had she lived a thousand years, she could not have surpassed this. Goethe's Iphigenia, the mature Woman, with its myriad delicate traits, never surpasses, scarcely equals, what we know of her in Euripides.

Can I appreciate this work in a translation ? I think so, impossible as it may seem to one who can enjoy the thousand melodies, and words in exactly the right place, and cadence of the original. They say you can see the Apollo Belvidere in a plaster cast, and I cannot doubt it, so great the benefit conferred on my mind by a transcript thus imperfect. And so with these translations from the Greek. I can divine the original through this veil, as I can see the movements of a spirited horse by those of his coarse grasscloth muffler. Besides, every translator who feels his subject is inspired, and the divine Aura informs even his stammering lips.

Iphigenia is more like one of the women Shakspeare loved than the others ; she is a tender virgin, ennobled and strengthened by sentiment more than intellect ; what they call a Woman *par excellence*.

Macaria is more like one of Massinger's women. She advances boldly, though with the decorum of her sex and nation :

" *Macaria.* Impute not boldness to me that I come
        Before you, strangers ; this my first request
        I urge ; for silence and a chaste reserve
        Is Woman's genuine praise, and to remain
        Quiet within the house. But I come forth,
        Hearing thy lamentations, Iolaus ;
        Though charged with no commission, yet perhaps
        I may be useful."   *   *

Her speech when she offers herself as the victim is reasonable, as one might speak to-day. She counts the cost all through. Iphigenia is too timid and delicate to dwell upon the loss of earthly bliss and the due experience of life, even as much as Jephtha's daughter did ; but Macaria is explicit, as well befits the daughter of Hercules.

" Should *these* die, myself
Preserved, of prosperous future could I form
One cheerful hope ?
A poor forsaken virgin who would deign
To take in marriage ? Who would wish for sons
From one so wretched ? Better then to die,
Than bear such undeserved miseries ;
One less illustrious this might more beseem.

*　　　*　　　*

I have a soul that unreluctantly
Presents itself, and I proclaim aloud
That for my brothers and myself I die.
I am not fond of life, but think I gain
An honorable prize to die with glory."

Still nobler when Iolaus proposes rather that she shall draw lots with her sisters.

" *By lot* I will not die, for to such death
No thanks are due, or glory — name it not.
If you accept me, if my offered life
Be grateful to you, willingly I give it
For these ; but by constraint I will not die."

Very fine are her parting advice and injunctions to them all :

" Farewell ! revered old man, farewell ! and teach
These youths in all things to be wise, like thee,
Naught will avail them more."

Macaria has the clear Minerva eye ; Antigone's is deeper and more capable of emotion, but calm ; Iphigenia's glistening, gleaming with angel truth, or dewy as a hidden violet.

I am sorry that Tennyson, who spoke with such fitness of all the others in his " Dream of fair Women," has not of Iphigenia. Of her alone he has not made a fit picture, but only of the circumstances of the sacrifice. He can never have taken to heart this work of Euripides, yet he was so worthy to feel it. Of Jephtha's daughter he has spoken as he would of Iphigenia, both in her beautiful song, and when

" I heard Him, for He spake, and grief became
    A solemn scorn of ills.

It comforts me in this one thought to dwell —
    That I subdued me to my father's will ;
Because the kiss he gave me, ere I fell,
    Sweetens the spirit still.

Moreover it is written, that my race
    Hewed Ammon, hip and thigh, from Arroer
Or Arnon unto Minneth. Here her face
    Glowed as I looked on her.

She locked her lips ; she left me where I stood ;
    ' Glory to God,' she sang, and past afar,
Thridding the sombre boskage of the woods,
    Toward the morning-star.''

In the " Trojan dames " there are fine touches of nature with regard to Cassandra. Hecuba shows that mixture of shame and reverence that prose kindred always do, towards the inspired child, the poet, the elected sufferer for the race.

When the herald announces that she is chosen to be the mistress of Agamemnon, Hecuba answers indignant, and betraying the involuntary pride and faith she felt in this daughter.

" The virgin of Apollo, whom the God,
    Radiant with golden locks, allowed to live
    In her pure vow of maiden chastity ?
Tal. With love the raptured virgin smote his heart.
Hec. Cast from thee, O my daughter, cast away
    Thy sacred wand ; rend off the honored wreaths,
    The splendid ornaments that grace thy brows.''

But the moment Cassandra appears, singing wildly her inspired song, Hecuba calls her

" My *frantic* child.''

Yet how graceful she is in her tragic phrenzy, the chorus shows —

" How sweetly at thy house's ills thou smilest,
    Chanting what haply thou wilt not show true ! ''

But if Hecuba dares not trust her highest instinct about her daughter, still less can the vulgar mind of the herald (a man not without tenderness of heart, but with no princely, no poetic blood) abide the wild, prophetic mood which insults his prejudices both as to country and decorums of the sex. Yet Agamemnon, though not a noble man, is of large mould, and could admire this strange beauty which excited distaste in common minds.

> " *Tal.* What commands respect, and is held high
>   As wise, is nothing better than the mean
>   Of no repute ; for this most potent king
>   Of all the Grecians, the much-honored son
>   Of Atreus, is enamored with his prize,
>   This frantic raver. I am a poor man,
>   Yet would I not receive her to my bed."

Cassandra answers, with a careless disdain,

> " This is a busy slave."

With all the lofty decorum of manners among the ancients, how free was their intercourse, man to man, how full the mutual understanding between prince and " busy slave ! " Not here in adversity only, but in the pomp of power it was so. Kings were approached with ceremonious obeisance, but not hedged round with etiquette ; they could see and know their fellows.

The Andromache here is just as lovely as that of the Iliad.

To her child whom they are about to murder, the same that was frightened at the " glittering plume," she says,

> " Dost thou weep,
>   My son ? Hast thou a sense of thy ill fate?
>   Why dost thou clasp me with thy hands, why hold
>   My robes, and shelter thee beneath my wings,
>   Like a young bird ? No more my Hector comes,
>   Returning from the tomb ; he grasps no more
>   His glittering spear, bringing protection to thee."
>
>   *   *   *   *   *
>   *   *   " O, soft embrace,
>   And to thy mother dear. O, fragrant breath !

> In vain I swathed thy infant limbs, in vain
> I gave thee nurture at this breast, and toiled,
> Wasted with care. *If ever*, now embrace,
> Now clasp thy mother ; throw thine arms around
> My neck, and join thy cheek, thy lips to mine.''

As I look up, I meet the eyes of Beatrice Cenci. Beautiful one ! these woes, even, were less than thine, yet thou seemest to understand them all. Thy clear, melancholy gaze says, they, at least, had known moments of bliss, and the tender relations of nature had not been broken and polluted from the very first. Yes ! the gradations of woe are all but infinite : only good can be infinite.

Certainly the Greeks knew more of real home intercourse and more of Woman than the Americans. It is in vain to tell me of outward observances. The poets, the sculptors, always tell the truth. In proportion as a nation is refined, women *must* have an ascendency. It is the law of nature.

Beatrice ! thou wert not " fond of life," either, more than those princesses. Thou wert able to cut it down in the full flower of beauty, as an offering to *the best* known to thee. Thou wert not so happy as to die for thy country or thy brethren, but thou wert worthy of such an occasion.

In the days of chivalry, Woman was habitually viewed more as an ideal ; but I do not know that she inspired a deeper and more home-felt reverence than Iphigenia in the breast of Achilles, or Macaria in that of her old guardian, Iolaus.

We may, with satisfaction, add to these notes the words to which Haydn has adapted his magnificent music in " The Creation.''

" In native worth and honor clad, with beauty, courage, strength adorned, erect to heaven, and tall, he stands, a Man ! — the lord and king of all ! The large and arched front sublime of wisdom deep declares the seat, and in his eyes with brightness shines the soul, the breath and image of his God. With fondness leans upon his breast the partner for him formed,— a woman fair, and graceful spouse. Her softly smiling virgin looks, of flowery spring the mirror, bespeak him love, and joy and bliss.''

Whoever has heard this music must have a mental standard as to what Man and Woman should be. Such was marriage in Eden, when " erect to heaven *he* stood ; " but since, like other institutions, this must be not only reformed, but revived, the following lines may be offered as a picture of something intermediate, — the seed of the future growth : —

H.

THE SACRED MARRIAGE.

And has another's life as large a scope ?
It may give due fulfilment to thy hope,
And every portal to the unknown may ope.

If, near this other life, thy inmost feeling
Trembles with fateful prescience of revealing
The future Deity, time is still concealing ;

If thou feel thy whole force drawn more and more
To launch that other bark on seas without a shore ;
And no still secret must be kept in store ;

If meannesses that dim each temporal deed,
The dull decay that mars the fleshly weed,
And flower of love that seems to fall and leave no seed —

Hide never the full presence from thy sight
Of mutual aims and tasks, ideals bright,
Which feed their roots to-day on all this seeming blight.

Twin stars that mutual circle in the heaven,
Two parts for spiritual concord given,
Twin Sabbaths that inlock the Sacred Seven ;

Still looking to the centre for the cause,
Mutual light giving to draw out the powers,
And learning all the other groups by cognizance of one another's
    laws.

The parent love the wedded love includes ;
The one permits the two their mutual moods ;
The two each other know, 'mid myriad multitudes ;

With child-like intellect discerning love,
And mutual action energizing love,
In myriad forms affiliating love.

A world whose seasons bloom from pole to pole,
A force which knows both starting-point and goal,
A Home in Heaven,— the Union in the Soul.